CW00521978

Inês, nicknamed Nish by her university friends, is a 23-year-old Swansea University psychology graduate with a big interest in food and cooking; this passion gave rise to *Nourish with Nish – The Complete Vegan Student Handbook.* Seven years ago, she took the decision to cut out meat from her diet, and four years later, the rest of all animal products followed: these were both controversial decisions under the roof of a Portuguese household but it motivated her to learn all about nutrition, how to stay healthy on a vegan diet and how to simplify a seemingly complicated lifestyle.

NOURISH

WITH NISH

The Complete Vegan
Student Handbook

Inês Teixeira-Dias

AUSTIN MACAULEY PUBLISHERS™

LONDON · CAMBRIDGE · NEW YORK · SHARJAH

A CIP catalogue record for this title is available from the British Library.

ISBN 9781788232500 (Paperback)
ISBN 9781784558895 (Hardback)
ISBN 9781849639668 (ePub e-book)

www.austinmacauley.com

First Published (2021)
Austin Macauley Publishers Ltd
25 Canada Square
Canary Wharf
London
E14 5LQ

ACKNOWLEDGEMENT

It's always a good idea to start with the truth. The truth is: I never intended on writing a book and I never dreamed of being capable of such a thing. I didn't have many inspirations for cooking and developing recipes (many were wonderful accidents in very messy university kitchens), but I would like to give a huge amount of thanks to those who supported me through life whilst I was busy behind the scenes putting random recipes into notebooks for no real reason and making a mess. It turned out pretty well! I feel deeply blessed to be surrounded by such patient and positive people – without you all, this book would not have come to fruition the way it has and for that I am truly grateful.

Dad – you have been indispensable to me since I first went vegetarian, almost 8 years ago now. Your interest in keeping me healthy, your care, your kindness and unconditional support has been invaluable to me over the years and I feel so fortunate for everything you have taught me about looking after myself. Look Mum, I made this! Can we put it on the fridge? Thank you for teaching me to stay true to myself and my beliefs, to be resilient and hard working. All of it was very needed when piecing together every bit of this book.

To my wonderful final year house: Ana, Maria, Jack and Freddie, where do I begin? To keep it short and sweet, you taught me the beauty of sharing food, cooking for others, cooking with others and the pleasure of enjoying a delicious meal sat around the table. Our very first and last memories as a house were around our kitchen table and I wouldn't have had it any other way. Thank you for putting up with all my incessant taste tastes, photo shoots and "has anyone got 5 minutes and a hand, literally, to spare?" 10/10 hand modelling from all of you!

Steph, my University boss: your pride in me strengthened the pride I have for myself and my work, you always helped me stay focused and feel supported every step of the way. I was never alone with you by my side. Thank you to Reeve, for never doubting my most ambitious ideas – you were always a voice of strength and reason for me (not to mention you and Julie formed the foundations of one of my favourite recipes in this book).

To Lina and Lucy, for always showing up at my door with huge smiles, huge hugs and a wonderfully empty stomach waiting to be filled. You helped ease the load of doing everything at once with your calmness, positivity and encouragement, and always filled our dinner times together with enough laughs to last a lifetime.

Inês e Tanta, vindo de uma cultura contra tudo que não seja comer um bom bife, o vosso apoio e interesse no meu trabalho e cozinha foi muito importante para mim. Nunca esquecerei o quão normal vocês me fizeram sentir no meio de tudo isto. Muito, muito, obrigada.

A Maria Maza, Maria Bardaji y Guille – fuisteis los primeros en probar mi comida fuera de mi país, ¡dándome la confianza de organizar una cena vegana con el resto de mi gente española! A Tété, Maria, Maria, Ana, Rocio, Marta y Begoña: estaba muy nerviosa el día que os hice una cena vegana, pero estoy increíblemente agradecida de que le dieseis una oportunidad (María Maza, a la próxima!). Incluso cuando pensabais que estaba loca, me apoyasteis de todas formas. Muchas gracias!

Finally, this message wouldn't be visible to you right now had it not been for the amazing team over at Austin Macauley taking a big risk on me and my work! I feel honoured to have had the opportunity to work with such a high-class team of professionals and I'm unbelievably appreciative of all the hard work, patience and effort it has taken to bring my book to life, even more so in the face of producing this during a global pandemic. Thank you to you all, from the bottom of my heart.

SYNOPSIS

"Nourish With Nish – The Ultimate Student Guide to going, and being, vegan (and a few extra student tips here and there)." My name is Inês. I'm a 23-year-old psychology graduate from Swansea University, and have a huge passion for the environment, nature and my health; all key motivators in me going vegan just over 4 years ago.

This book was written throughout my final year of being vegan as a student, on a student budget, on a student schedule, and in line with the student mentality, based on personal experience. It runs through how to transition into going vegan, how to maintain a vegan diet at university and a host of various other student hacks and tips on how to be the best student you can possibly be. It aims to inspire and guide students who would like to go vegan but have no idea where to begin to take the step.

This book is divided into various sections; tips on the transition, general tips for cooking and kitchen etiquette, 'vegan myths, debunked', and tips on student life (budgeting, time management, studying, managing stress, best student apps), how to read food labels, a kitchen packing list and a complete step by step guide to going vegan. Following this comes 65 recipes.

Having been vegan as a student at university for three years, and for some time during secondary school, my experience with regards to the challenges one faces when going vegan, isn't unique. Every single vegan will regularly be asked where they get their protein from, and every time this question is answered, the person is always left in shock that vegans thrive. However, I am able to offer practical solutions that I have learned over the years, in dealing with the day to day encounters of being a vegan. From what to do with tofu, to eating out as a vegan, and of course, how to still eat vegan after a student night out.

Overall, this handy guide is a must-have for anyone considering going vegan and just needs that little push. It doesn't necessarily have to just apply to students; anyone on a budget looking for quick and easy recipes can benefit from this book.

Nourish With Nish – The Ultimate Student Guide to Going, and Being, Vegan and a Few Extra Student Tips Here and There.

My name is Inês, nicknamed Nish by my university friends, and I'm a 23-year-old student who has been vegan for four years, vegetarian for two years before that. This book is the ultimate guide to going, being and staying vegan. Everything from snacks and desserts (no skimping!) to how to make sure you're getting all your nutrients and a few vegan tips and tricks I've learnt along the way to keep you happy, healthy and most importantly; stuffed.

According to The Vegan Society, *'demand for meat-free food increased by 987% in 2017'* (Just Eat, 2018). The sheer amount of information and available education on the effects of meat and dairy consumption on the environment, animal welfare and physical and mental health has generated huge global interest in veganism. Clear skin, a naturally regulated weight, reducing your carbon footprint, saving the animals, who wouldn't want it all? Eating right is a form of respecting your body and looking after it is important to make sure you see as many full and bountiful years as possible, without having to spend years eating grass, contrary to popular belief.

In this book, it's simple; I'll be giving you a guide on how to go vegan, basic cooking tips and recipes for three meals of the day, sure to fill you and feed you for days. Remember that food is more than just something to fill your stomach; it builds your body, your mind and regulates your mood. In this book, breakfast is designed to be prepared quickly and give you enough fuel for those dreaded 9am's; lunches are designed as takeaway-able (e.g. in a box/wrapper up) and dinner, something hot you can eat on a plate and be shared easily (should you want to) to add a little comfort to your life. Most importantly, what food you can get on your way home from the kebab shop after your night out. Student essentials. Priorities!

Tips and Notes on Veganism (full guide further down)

1. Don't do it overnight. This can be seriously damaging to your body and will leave you tired and probably very hungry; that's not what we vegans are about! Start by reducing consumption of meats and dairy. Conquer a meal/a food a month, for example. Start by vegan breakfasts and snacks. Then once that becomes habits, move on to lunch.

2. Read into why so many people are doing it in the first place. What does animal agriculture do to the environment? What are the effects of consuming dairy on the body, both positive and negative? Can those positives be reached with plant-based alternatives? Education is your power here. Watch documentaries (e.g. What The Health, Earthlings, Cowspiracy, Forks Over Knives, The Game Changers), and read articles; The internet is bursting with them. Opinions presenting both sides to the story. Almond milk takes 1000 litres of water to produce 1 litre of milk, so consider oat milk (the most sustainable out of all plant-based milks). However soya tends to have the most protein.

3. Veganism is a little tricky when getting started. Lots of new ingredients, cooking methods and making sure you're still healthy. But once you know and learn how to cook, what your body runs well off and what it doesn't, it becomes second nature, just like what you're doing now. Having trained your mind and your body to know what works, it's like anything else; it just takes practise. Doesn't mean it has to be hard or laborious, but you are probably eating and cooking every day anyway, so nothing should change too much.

4. Going vegan forces you to cook with ingredients you've never heard of. Cornflour, nutritional yeast, apple cider vinegar, what even are those? Your new best friends! Cooking is a life skill, an impressive one and one necessary for your survival. It's a big adaptation process, but once it's habit it's easy.

5. We should all care more about the animals around us, about the environment we live in, about our bodies. There is no Planet B. The thickest of arctic ice has cracked and this is on the verge of being irreversible damage to our planet; whilst the climate is constantly changing, the rate at which humans are consuming the planet's resources is alarming, and sooner or later the planet simply won't be able to keep up. We are living terrifically unsustainably, and whilst plant-based diets don't offer all the answers, they're an excellent start.

6. Look after your body. Students have a tendency to neglect health

because we want cheap and quick solutions to a lifestyle, unless it involves alcohol. In which case, many of us have no problem spending £30 a night on alcohol and writing off the entire following day to feel sorry for ourselves eating take-away on the sofa with our housemates zooming in on our friends' faces on Snapchat to pass the day away. There's nothing wrong with enjoying a drink every now and then, but if you're chugging 10 pints a night, three times a week, this might show a little more sign of damage than your hangover the next morning. In a few years' time, it will inevitably catch up with you. The same with your food; if you're eating take-way every time you try and cure a hangover, that's going to catch up with you, not least to mention the dent it'll leave in your wallet! Everything you ate as a child built the adult you are today. Everything you're doing now as a young adult has the power to shape the older adult you become. When followed well, veganism prioritises your health and what you put in is exactly what you get out.

7. Don't be too hard on yourself. It can be a difficult journey to get started on, but it's worth it. Don't be put off by the overwhelming things you feel you need to do to go vegan. Step by step, day by day, you'll get there, if it's what you want. And if it's not, at least you've learned a hell of a lot along the way and are more equipped to have open conversations about veganism with those around you and make more informed decisions about your consumption.

8. There's a vegan option for everything nowadays and it's often just as tasty. Chocolate fudge cake, katsu curry, sweet and sour Chinese, cheeseburgers; you name it. There has never been a better time to be vegan and we are spoiled for choice on meat-free alternatives. Almost every supermarket nowadays offers them; it's a question of familiarising yourself with products and knowing how to cook them. Tofu is bland, let's not lie. But marinate it in some soy sauce and ginger? You've got yourself an incredible base for a stir fry, a sandwich or filler for a salad.

9. A huge element to succeeding as a vegan is planning ahead.
Knowing what vegetables you've got. If your days are busier, you'll need more food. If it's going to be a hot sunny day, you might not fancy that bowl of steaming hot food, but might prefer a salad. Be ready for yourself.

10. Shop wisely. If you only buy vegan products, you'll only use vegan products. Shopping towards the end of the day, in many supermarkets, will mean you find loads of reduced-price products. Don't shop when you're hungry; buy in bulk. You can never have too much pasta or rice!

Top Tips for Cooking

1. Always read the recipe through from start to finish first. It will give you a visual idea of what you'll be doing, and you may be met with a surprise later on if you haven't read the whole thing through first.

2. Make sure you have everything you need, but bear in mind it's often easy to improvise.

3. Start by preparing all your vegetables first so that when it comes to cooking, you're not faffing about because you forgot to dice that carrot; you just want to eat! Get straight to it. Work efficiently and enjoy your food sooner (and hopefully not burnt).

4. How to test if potatoes are boiled; stick a knife into a piece of potentially boiled potato. If it separates/slides off the knife easily, it's ready. Mash, here you come!

5. The first shop of the year is often the most expensive; condiments, spices, kitchenware – it all adds up. But it'll last you and is cheap to replace bit by bit when it runs out. Don't be put off! Great things are headed your way (particularly in the form of stuffed sweet peppers and vegan brownies).

6. Buy in bulk where you can. I bought 300g of Paprika online for the same price as a small jar of it at the supermarket, and it lasted me so much longer. Ten times the weight for the same price! Every penny matters as a student, so invest wisely.

7. Buy low-sodium soy sauce if you can. As a vegan, you use a fair bit of it (not just in Asian-style recipes), and it all adds up. University stress will raise your blood pressure enough!

8. Veganism, like many things in life, is about consistency and sustainability; eating one meal a week that is purely protein packed is probably going to leave you protein deficient. Don't make one fancy meal every three days if it sucks the life out of you. Plan, prepare and thrive.

9. Your food, after cooking, is likely to be a little too hot to eat immediately. Quickly do your washing up whilst it cools down to the perfect temperature. Everything will scrub off easily, and by the time you're done, your kitchen is clean, and your food is at the perfect temperature to eat!

10. Blunt knife? No problem. Turn a plate or a bowl upside down on a work surface. Around the circular rim in the centre of the plate, place the blade at a flat diagonal against the edge and sharpen the knife blade gently.

11. Don't hold back on the olive oil; us Mediterraneans aren't famous for our diet for nothing! Don't skimp on it. It adds wonderful textures and flavours to food and comes with an abundance of health benefits.

12. Things to do whilst you wait for your vegetables to roast/food to cook;

do your reading for tomorrow's lecture, write your essay plan, do that maths problem you left behind, chuck a wash in, do last night's washing up if you didn't get a chance to do it, check in on your housemates, put some music on and have a dance party for one, decide what you're going to wear for your night out later, read a magazine.

13. An alternative way to use a sieve if you don't want to transfer the contents of what is in your pan out of it. Hold the pan in one hand and the sieve in the other. Place the sieve directly on top of the pan, like a sealing lid (with the dip facing down, not up, so there should be no dome). Firmly hold the sieve on top and drain the liquid out.

14. If you don't fancy cooking an entire meal from scratch, the classics can also be made quickly and effectively; sausages with mash (peas and gravy!), meat-free breaded fillets with vegetables and rice/pasta; don't forget all those things exist. Ease the load for when time is a little tighter. Carrots and hummus as a snack don't need a recipe, neither does pasta with sauce from a jar (dairy-free pesto; own brand tomato sauces are often vegan), but it's all still there. Don't forget!

15. Looking to add texture to a soup? As your soup cooks, gently fry some small pieces of onion until crisp. Chuck in when plating up into a bowl! If you're looking to pack in more vegetables, wilt in some spinach after blending the soup.

16. Before squeezing a lemon, roll it on your work surface using your hand, particularly the heel of your palm. It'll make it much easier to juice and means you can get the most out of it for your meals.

17. If you finish a jar of sundried tomatoes, keep the leftover oil in the fridge. It makes a great salad dressing and adds extra flavour to dishes.

18. How to slice and dice an onion: the top, pointy bit, of an onion is called the stem, the bottom of an onion is called the root. Lay the onion on a chopping board and slice it in half, running directly through the stem and the root (as if you're drawing a line between them with your knife). Once you've got two halves, peel them. To dice it, lie a half flat on a chopping board and cut inwards towards the root at varying levels. They are your horizontal cuts. Then, cut vertically down from one side of the onion to the other, with the tip of your knife pointing towards the root. Finally, dice the onion by chopping vertically with the tip of your knife pointing away from the root.

19. Italians say that when boiling pasta, the water should be as salty as the sea. Don't hold back! Pasta water can also be used to thin out sauces.

20. When cooking rice, thoroughly wash it to remove all the starch. Wash until any water runs clear.

<u>Vegan Myths Debunked</u>

You will encounter plenty of people who will turn into fully trained nutritionists and animal activists on the spot after hearing you are vegan. As much as it may be your natural instinct to react, these conversations don't have to be a source of conflict; they can be a source of education and healthy debate.

1. "But…where do you get your protein from?" Soy milk. Lentils. Pulses. Beans; black, pinto, butter, kidney, borlotti, edamame, black-eyed, cannellini; the possibilities are endless. Tofu. Sweet potato. Peas. Rice. Quinoa. Shall I keep going? Concern yourself more with vitamins, like B12, that are a little harder to get. But even then, most dairy-free milks and butters are fortified with added B12 vitamins. Two slices of toast during the day, milk in your breakfast, maybe in the afternoon too if you're feeling adventurous, and you're covered. Protein won't be an issue, as long as you're eating consistently. Read food labels to learn what vitamins and minerals are inside.

2. "But…cheese." Okay, I'll admit. It tastes great. But the dairy industry and the meat industry go hand in hand in terms of ethical practices. Thankfully, vegan cheeseboards are now a thing and if you really want some dairy cheese, it's not the end of the world.

3. "I could never be vegan." You probably could, you're just unfamiliar with the process and afraid of change. But just because you can't commit to being 100% vegan or just because you can't do everything, doesn't mean you should do nothing. Everybody can do something. Start small and build it into your life. Even if it's just a small handful of changes. The same way you've learned to integrate the foods you now eat into your life; you can learn and teach yourself a new life too.

4. "We need animals to survive! We've always eaten them!" Yes, in an environment where animal agriculture wasn't the leading cause of climate change (more than all global public transport **combined**). We need protein to survive. Calcium, vitamins, minerals. But they don't have to come from animals, nowadays. We no longer live in an environment where eating meat is essential for survival.

5. "You're not killing any animals for milk or eggs, so what's the big deal?" The meat industry is the dairy industry; the two work hand in hand. Anything factory farmed or produced on a mass scale is not done pleasantly, as it has to be quick and financially feasible. You're not a baby

cow. If I were to give your puppy human milk for him to grow, would you find that weird? Probably! The same way: it's a little odd, when you think about it, that it's been normalised for humans to drink the milk of another species that isn't our own. Calcium is important, but the industry has got us vegans covered. For example, flour in the UK is fortified (by law) with calcium, iron and other vitamins. The darker and leafier your vegetables, the higher its calcium content. Plant-based milks have added calcium and vitamins to ensure that you're healthy!

6. "I would never eat dog, they're different. You can't compare them to cows." They're extremely similar animals, but your culture teaches you that some animals are to be domesticated as pets, some are to be eaten, and some are to be wild. But really, the only thing that divides these animals is your perspective towards them. Ultimately, they all raise families, feel pain, feel joy and are sentient living beings. Have you seen those videos on the internet of cows in fields chasing after footballs? They're basically huge grass puppies.

7. "Plants have feelings too!" Run across your lawn and tell me if it screams.

Student Life – Tips and Tricks

Budgeting Tips

- Learning to budget can be a painful process, and sometimes leave you in the red, asking to be saved by the Bank of Mum and Dad. But this doesn't always have to be the case, especially if other options aren't available to you. Learn where to spend your pennies, shop around and shop wisely. Don't buy more than you need and always shop with a list! If you're really keen, keep track of your finances, either with an app or with a simple excel spreadsheet. That will often do the trick.

- If you're able to balance both your studies/social life and a job at university, I would recommend it. It eases the psychological stress of finances and puts money into perspective. Want to buy x? That's 4 hours' worth of work! Worth it? Maybe not… Prioritise food; it gives you the energy and motivation you need to face those late-night library sessions, the fact that eduroam is down, and all other student nags. Stay calm. It'll be okay (mainly because you've got a delicious brownie in your bag). Your body needs fuel, and you shouldn't hold back from giving it everything it needs to thrive – veganism isn't a fad diet.

- Buy and cook in bulk. Dried/canned/frozen ingredients are ideal. As a vegan, obviously a lot of our food is fresh, however some things can be well substituted for frozen, for example spinach/berries – it's often also cheaper than buying fresh.

- Refrigerate or freeze portions for later on. If you're short on fridge/freezer space, share a meal with a friend, and set up a deal where you make one then they make another, and you alternate. This is also a great way to add some structure into your daily routine, and it's a pleasant experience cooking with others/allowing others to cook for you.

- Plan your meals for the week and organise a shopping list before you go shopping. Don't go without an idea of what to get, otherwise you'll over-shop, over-spend, and won't eat the food you bought in the time it'll give you to stay fresh! Reduce food waste by sticking to a plan.

- Top tip: if you're tempted to buy something a little pricey, picture the following. Someone is giving you what you're about to buy in one hand, and in the other hand is the amount of money it's worth in cash. Which one would you pick? If the answer is the latter, don't buy it!

Time Management/Studying

- Only keep one diary; pick a layout that you like with enough space to manage all your activities. Writing things down is the new trying to remember them!
- Use lists (even if they start with 'write a list'). Don't make them too long; it'll demotivate you to complete them, so keep them relatively basic but include all the essentials.
- Cut departmental deadlines short on a personal level. This way you can allow time for any unexpected emergencies to interfere, and if you manage to get it done on time then you can sit back and relax without having to be involved in the last minute panic of your course. Avoid your course group chat at all costs. The person that didn't turn up to any lectures is starting to panic and you don't need that in your life.
- Don't believe everything you read on your halls/course group chats. Word gets around quickly, and group chats suffer terribly from Chinese Whispers. So specifically, in terms of deadlines etc, if you're unsure then email your module leader, student experience team, Head of Department (if necessary) or a close friend of yours you know is trustworthy and reliable.
- Always email yourself a copy of your work/store it on iCloud/memory stick/external hard drive. Nothing worse than slaving away on an assignment, only to realise in the midst of it all you forgot to save it and now it's gone. It happens, and don't assume it'll only happen to others!
- When studying, put your phone on Hold. Download the app, and compete with your friends at your university and others to see who can rack up the greatest number of points on the app. These points can then be transferred into real life into things like free coffees etc, so it is worth investing in for the sake of your studies and your lifestyle!
- Revision: study topics in short chunks and multiple times, as opposed to large chunks just the once. Past papers, just like in your GCSEs/A Levels, are essential and should always form part of your exam preparation. It's all fun and games knowing the theory but if you can't apply it to get the marks then it's worthless.
- If you tend to suffer from terrible exam stress, contact your examining body, e.g. your school/university exams department, and get in touch to organise alternative arrangements, should you feel you need them. They are there to help, and truly want you to do your best. It can be intensely off-putting, being sat in a hall with 600 other students, so if you feel it would be better to be sat in a room with just 10 others then get organised,

get in touch and make it happen. Don't make exams any harder than they have to be. You're under enough stress already! Your Students' Union will also be able to offer a range of support. Reach out, they can help.

- Plan your question in the exam. Sat down, your thoughts are cloudy and seeing things written in front of you can more easily trigger other thoughts, as well as ensure you're less likely to forget them. Say what you have to say!

- Don't spend time with people that make you feel more stressed/anxious/depressed during exams. Everybody deals with these periods differently, and your studies are your number one priority.

- You can spend all the time in the world revising, however, work smarter; not necessarily harder. Find what works for you; post it notes, mind maps, notes, voice notes, reciting, highlighting; whatever it might be. The more confident you are in your material, the less likely you'll feel panicked in exams.

- Some things are out of your control; if the exam doesn't go to plan or as well as you had expected, pick yourself back up and work towards bouncing back from it; it's no longer in your control. Whether that be changing your study method for the next exam or retaking the module, there's always a solution and a way to improve.

- Eat well! The brain is responsible for 25% of the body's metabolic consumption, and this increases drastically during exams in revision (every wondered why you're always hungry when revising?). Fuel yourself. You need it.

- Never work with your laptop plugged in. Start with it fully charged, and when it dies, it's time for you to take a break and get moving. Get up, go outside, take a walk, do some washing, cook a meal, take a break. When your laptop is recharged and so are you, get straight back to it.

Managing Stress

- Most people, at one point or another, will feel stressed. Whether they study, work or neither, our environments are full of little niggles, and in the case of students, rather big ones. You might not be able to change what happens to you, but you can always change how you react to it.
- Symptoms of stress can manifest itself in a number of ways, but the most common to all would be anxiety, headaches, changes in appetite, difficulties sleeping, irritability and isolation. Learn to recognise these symptoms and learn what works for you to relieve stress. Walks, exercise, drawing, reading for pleasure, music, yoga; you do you.
- University can be a terribly isolating and lonely time for some, so don't feel the pressure to be having 'the best time of your life'. There's a lot to adjust to, and yes, you may be surrounded by people all the time, but you'll find a lot of them won't know you the way your friends at home do. Some people ooze positive energies, and you click with them instantly. Prioritise them and be around people who are good for you. Don't just hang out with people good for your mental health, be someone who is good for your own mental health.
- Go for a walk, get some fresh air, sit on a bench outside the library, walk up and away from your desk for a while, get some snacks, designate a certain working environment to your studies.
- It's better not to mix living and studying environments together. You should come home at the end of the day and enjoy the space you live in to relax and unwind, as opposed to coming home and studying in your room, for hours to come. Separate the environments so mentally you're able to distinguish between the two and prepare appropriately.
- Both your university and Students' Union will offer support on various levels. Chaplaincy, counselling, stress management courses. Get talking, investigate and see what you can find to help you. Let others help you, and don't be afraid to acknowledge when there's a problem.

Best Student Apps

- Hold: convert time off your phone into points and real-life prizes! Beat your friends, get free coffees, reduce your screen time and increase your productivity. Study app where you 'lock' your phone; the longer your phone is on hold, the more points you accumulate, which can be translated into free things in life. We all know students love a freebie.

Android; Self Control for Study. Similar principle that allows you to block access to certain social media sites for a predesignated period of time.
- Timer+: an app that allows you to set multiple timers; label each one, reuse each one/set them down to the second etc. Perfect for cooking those slightly more complex dishes.
- Habit Streak (android only); trying to establish a new habit, e.g. eating breakfast every morning? This will keep you on track. Monitor your progress on establishing new habits! Productive – habit tracker (iOS); track 5 habits for free.
- Evernote; keep all your lecture notes, shopping lists and to-do lists stored safely online.
- Urbanspoon; restaurant finder based on location, prices and type of cuisine served.
- Daily water; don't forget to stay hydrated! Set regular reminders on your phone to drink water and track your intake.

Reading Food Labels

Traps in Food Labelling

- Just because something is labelled as low fat; beware, as it'll often be high in sugar to 'compensate'.
- Companies label portion sizes very strangely. Beware, as they may cite a certain number of grams, however, under further inspection, you see this is only half a normal portion size, etc.
- Reduced fat is not the same as low fat. Reduced can still be elevated! If this concerns you, always read the label. What counts as high/low levels?

Element	High	Low	Recommendations
Sugars	> 22.5g per 100	< 5g per 100	70g M, 50g W
Salt	> 1.5g per 100	< 0.3g per 100	6g both
Total fat	> 17.5g per 100	< 3g per 100	80g M, 65g W
Saturated fat	> 5g per 100	< 1.5g per 100	25g or less M, 20g or less W

- Just because something isn't labelled as vegan, doesn't mean it's not. A lot of companies, legally, are not allowed to label it as such, due to cross contamination reasons, e.g. if a product is produced in the same environment/factory as another which actively contains animal products, they cannot guarantee no cross contamination. This is often primarily for people with allergies, to learn to read labels. Allergens are always listed in bold, e.g. milk, eggs.

- Fruit and vegetables portions explained:

Fruit	Veg
Apple – 1 medium	Aubergine – 1/3 aubergine
Apricot – 3 dried	Broccoli – 2 spears
Avocado – half	Brussel sprouts – 8
Banana – 1 medium	Cabbage – 2 handfuls sliced/ 1/6 small cabbage
Blackcurrants – 1 good handful	Carrots – 3 heaped tbsp sliced
Blueberries – 2 handfuls	Cauliflower – 8 florets
Fruit juice – 1 x 150ml	Celery – 3 sticks
Grapes – 1 handful	Chickpeas – 3 heaped tbsp
Kiwi – 2 fruits	Courgettes – half large
Mango – 2 slices (5cm/2inch slices)	Cucumber – 5 cm or 2-inch piece
Orange – 1 fruit	Lentils – 3 tbsp
Pineapple – 1 large slice	Lettuce – 1 cereal bowl
Plum – 2 medium	Mushrooms – 14 button mushrooms
Strawberries – 7 strawberries	Onion – 1 medium
Raspberries – 2 handfuls	Peas – 3 heaped tbsp
	Pepper – half
	Baby sweetcorn – 6 baby corn
	Canned sweetcorn – 3 heaped tbsp
	Tomato – 7 cherry / 1 large

Laundry Guide

 Machine wash

 Hand wash

 Do not wash

 Do not wring

 Do not dryclean

 Do not bleach

 Water temperature 30°C

 Water temperature 40°C

 Water temperature 50°C

 Water temperature 30°C

 Water temperature 40°C

 Water temperature 50°C

 Low temperature

 Medium temperature

 High temperature

 Iron

 Do not iron

 No steam

 Tumble dry

 Low heat

 Medium heat

 High heat

 Dry flat

 Dry in the shade

 Hang to dry

 Drip dry

Getting Food as a Vegan after a Night Out

- Chips are a solid base, but thankfully, there are many quick and easy ways to jazz them up.
- Base: chips. Many curry sauces at kebab shops are vegan (ask!!), as they're based on coconut milk, and then spiced. Gravy is less often vegan, but always worth asking anyway.
- Many veggie burgers also double up as vegan; again, just ask.
- Falafel and hummus wraps are common to Middle Eastern cuisine. So many kebab shops do them!
- Baked beans on chips; salad is plentiful; jacket potatoes!

Kitchen Packing List (aside from Standard Crockery)

- Garlic mincer
- Vegetable peeler
- Chopping knives
- Chopping board
- Cup measurement set
- Wooden spoon
- Measuring jug
- Steaming basket
- Saucepan (with high sides)
- Saucepan (with low sides)
- Blender
- Mixing bowl
- Small ovenproof dish
- Roasting tray
- Tin opener
- Grater (normally used for cheese, but here it's used for vegetables)
- Sieve
- Metal/glass straws

A complete Guide to going Vegan

1. Do it step by step. Go pescatarian, then vegetarian, then dairy free, then vegan! There's no rush though. It took me two years to go from pescatarian to vegan, but I got there, and I got there well! Make small changes to your day and build it up. I did it by conquering a meal at a time, starting with breakfast. I made all my breakfasts vegan, only bought plant-based milks and products, and once that became a solid habit and I was comfortable, I moved onto the next meal.

2. Veganism is all about knowledge. But once you know what you're doing, it's like second nature. The same way you can learn to cook with meat and dairy, you can learn to cook without it! Over your journey to transition into going vegan, you're going to be learning lots. Find excitement in what you're making, and work with flavours that are best for you. Experiment, and whilst along the way, you might make some questionable meals. Use what you know to improve them and make them work for you. Research online, read books, reach out to the vegan community on Instagram with your questions, speak to your vegan/vegetarian friends, read vegan blogs online. You have so much information at your fingertips, so use it to your advantage!

3. If you're going to commit, do it properly. Don't deprive your body of essential nutrients, so learn what your body needs and how much of it. In the first few months of going vegan, go to the doctors for blood tests regularly to make sure your body is adapting well and healthy on the inside. As soon as you've established yourself in your new lifestyle, you won't need to go as often.

4. Remember why you're doing it. There will probably come a time when you lose touch with why you started all of this in the first place. Being committed to change, like with anything, takes energy, and if you feel like you're losing your focus but want to keep going with it, re-watch some documentaries exposing the dairy/meat/food industry/impacts of eating meat on the environment etc. What The Health, Earthlings, Cowspiracy, OMG GMO, Forks Over Knives, The Game Changers or read The China Study, the world's largest and most comprehensive long term study on health.

5. Don't be too hard on yourself. If during your transition, you're really craving something and you really, really feel like you can't fill it with a vegan substitute, listen to your body. Your body needs salt, sugar, fat; all of these things. What it doesn't necessarily need is for those things to come from animal origins. There are plenty of vegan junk foods to eat nowadays, so

you shouldn't be short of options. Don't be too hard on yourself, either. It's better to be vegan 3/4 of the time than not at all. You're not a terrible person if you 'slip up'. It's better to have loads of imperfect vegans than a small handful of strict ones!

6. Planning is key. Being vegan teaches you excellent organisation. Collect a handful of recipes you're able to prepare well and that satisfy your needs in terms of protein, calcium, iron, B12, etc. Master these, and then expand your horizons! It's a continuous journey.

7. Veganism is not about cutting anything out. For everything you 'remove', you must substitute it with something equally as appropriate.

8. You will receive criticism. You will receive support and admiration. Learn to deal with both to your advantage. People criticise what they don't understand. Don't concern yourself with what other people eat, unless they come to you asking for help. They can do them, you do you. Don't judge others – it doesn't look good on anybody and gives you a reputation for being the 'angry vegan'.

9. Learn to read labels. There's an awful lot of ingredients that you'd be surprised are unnecessary in foods, but nonetheless are present. Any allergens, e.g. dairy, are often written in bold writing. In the UK, many labels will read 'may contain…'. This just declares the possibility that as the product is made in an environment where allergens are present, for allergy sufferers, for example it may not be safe to risk the cross contamination. However, in terms of active ingredients in the product, many animal derivatives may not have been used at all. It's simply a legality.

10. Veganism, unless it stems from an allergy, is a privileged choice and conscious decision. You will find some people will heavily criticise this decision but you know better than them your reasons and motivations for seeing this through. Don't worry about what others have to say about what you decide to eat or not.

11. The vast majority of your favourite meals can be 'veganised'. It's all in the research!

12. Change the way you shop; you will learn how many vegetables you eat, how much fruit you eat, and it's handy that many vegan staples are dried and can live on shelves, e.g. grains, beans, nuts etc. Buy in bulk where you can, and if you live near a local market, pop over in the last hour or so, when prices are reduced.

13. Eating out as a vegan: in the UK, many restaurants now do vegan cheeses for pizzas and there are normally always a few vegan options. Zizzi's has an entire vegan menu, as does Wetherspoons. Pizza Express, Wagamama, GBK, The Handmade Burger Co., Byron Burgers, Carluccio's,

Firezza Pizza, Las Iguanas, Giraffe, Yo! Sushi, Ask Italian, Toby Carvery, Nando's, Prezzo; the list goes on. If you're at a restaurant where you're unsure, there's no harm in asking. If they don't have a made plate, learn how to make one yourself. Pasta with roasted vegetables/tomato sauces, steamed vegetables with rice/sauces, remove ingredients and replace them with others they may have that are suitable for you. Don't be afraid to ask!

14. There's no way to be the perfect vegan. The point of veganism isn't to live perfectly; it's to live with purpose and intent, and to do what you can, within your means. You're already ahead of everybody else who are not even trying!

15. Frozen veggies are just as good as fresh! Same with fruits. Many supermarkets, nowadays, offer bags of prepared frozen and fresh veggies. Downside; they're packaged in plastic. But weigh up the pros and cons. Got a small fridge/limited space at university? Make use of the freezer and buy frozen veg/buy fresh vegetables, and prepare it and freeze it yourself.

16. Some vegan foods, like tofu and jackfruit, are naturally bland. The best way to add flavour is to marinate. Leave them to soak in soy sauce and ginger or lemon juice and garlic: done!

17. Veganism is not a weight loss plan. It is not a diet and should not be used as an excuse to restrict your eating, strictly count calories or give you a stronger sense of control over food. If you feel vulnerable with food or eating, and want to turn vegan to justify not eating certain things, veganism is not the answer at this time in your life. Strengthen a healthy relationship with your body and mind, it's the only thing you're guaranteed to have until the day you die. Look after it and it will, in turn, look after you. It's a cycle. You get what you give. Don't get too caught up in rules and 'restrictions' to the point of feeling anxious. Learn to love what you eat and what you can make.

Sources of….

- Calcium: dark green leafy vegetables (the darker and leafier it tends to be, the higher its calcium content), oranges, calcium fortified milks/dairy-free butters, etc. Flour, used in cereals and bread, in the UK, is fortified by law with various minerals, including calcium, iron and thiamine.
- Iron: spinach, dried fruits, oats, chickpeas.
- Zinc: lentils, tofu, seeds and nuts, e.g. pumpkin, almonds.
- Omega-3: walnuts, hemp seed, flax meal.

- Vitamin D: fortified soy/rice/oat milk, fortified cereals, mushrooms, sunshine!
- Vitamin B12: eat fortified foods at least twice a day, and consider a B12 supplement, particularly when you first go vegan.

Cup Conversion Chart

Cup Measurement	Millilitres (ml)
1 cup	250
3/4 cup	180
2/3 cup	160
1/2 cup	125
1/3 cup	80
1/4 cup	60
1 tbsp	15
1 tsp	5

Contents Page

Breakfast

1. Porridge...32
2. Chocolate Overnight Oats.................................32
3. Thick Pancakes..34
4. Thin Pancakes...36
5. Tofu Scramble...38
6. French Toast Sandwich...................................40
7. Nice Cream...42
8. Chia Seed Pudding..44
9. Beetroot Smoothie Bowl................................46
10. Vegan Full English (with a meat substitute)........48
11. Vegan Breakfast (without a meat substitute)........50

Lunch

1. Green and Grape Salad....................................54
2. Mediterranean Pasta Salad..............................56
3. Sandwich/Pitta Bread Fillings:.........................58
    a. Butter Bean and Avocado 58
    b. Mashed Avocado and Maple Fried Tofu..........60
    c. Vegan BLT...62
    d. Red Pesto and BBQ Tofu............................64
4. Wrap Fillings:
    a. Broccoli and Apple....................................66
    b. Smashed Sweet Potato and Black Bean..........68
    c. Fajitas..70
5. Apple and Beetroot Salad................................72
6. Bean Pastry Pockets.......................................74
7. Red Pesto Pasta with Black Olives and Spinach.......76
8. Rainbow Buddha Bowl....................................78
9. Pasta e Fagioli..80
10. Lemon and Garlic Jackfruit (with spinach and rice)......82

Dinner

1. Chilli Con Sausage Stew.................................. 86
2. Sweet Potato and Spinach Curry.......................88
3. Black Bean and Butternut Squash Curry..............90
4. Mushroom and Kale 'Stew'..............................92

5. Sweet and Sour Tofu/Meat-free Chicken................................94
6. Shepherd's Pie..96
7. Stuffed Peppers (with sweet potato mash, caramelised onions and sweetcorn)..98
8. Turmeric Rice Burrito Bowl..100
9. Spaghetti Bolognese..102
10. Jack's 'Cheesy' Vegetable Pasta....................................104
11. Mediterranean Tartlets...106
12. Jacket Sweet Potato, Hummus and Spinach....................108
13. Pea and Walnut Pesto..110
14. Broccoli and Mushroom Noodles...................................112
15. Lemon and Crispy Smoked Tofu Pasta...........................114
16. Garlic and Sweet Chilli Stir Fry.....................................116
17. Tomato Rice and Beans, Caramelised Onions and Tofu....118
18. Pea and Mushroom Risotto..120
19. Ratatouille...122
20. Lasagne..124

Soups

1. White: Chickpea...128
2. Red: Red Pepper and Tomato..130
3. Orange: Carrot and Ginger...132
4. Green: Pea and Mint...134
5. Pink: Kidney Bean..136

Sides

1. Balsamic Vinegar Roasted Mushrooms............................140
2. Sticky Pulled Carrots..142
3. Steamed Rice...144
4. Roast Dinner Stuffing..146
5. Paprika Roasted Potatoes..148
6. Sweet Potato and Rosemary/Thyme Wedges....................150
7. Boil and Bake Wedges...152
8. Beetroot and Orange Salad..154
9. White Bean and Avocado side Salad...............................156
10. Hummus..158

Desserts

1. Brownies...162
2. Chocolate Tofu Pudding.....................................164
3. Crumble..166
4. Grilled Cinnamon Pineapple Slices and Ice Cream.................168
5. Banana Muffins...170

Smoothies

1. White: Peanut Butter and Banana........................174
2. Red: Red Berry..174
3. Orange: Peach and Ginger..................................174
4. Green: Apple and Spinach..................................174
5. Purple: Blueberry...174

BREAKFAST

1. Porridge
2. Chocolate Overnight Oats
3. Thick Pancakes and Thin Pancakes
4. Tofu Scramble
5. French Toast Sandwich
6. Nice Cream
7. Chia Seed Pudding
8. Beetroot Smoothie Bowl
9. Vegan Full English (With a Meat substitute)
10. Vegan Breakfast (Without a Meat substitute)

Porridge

Ingredients

1/2 cup oats
1 cup milk
1 tsp cinnamon/cocoa powder
Dark chocolate (optional)
Frozen berries/banana/raisins/apple/chopped walnuts/dairy-free
yoghurt/desiccated coconut (toppings)

Recipe

1. Add the oats and milk into a pan, and mix. If using cocoa powder, use a fork to whisk it into the liquid, and further add any flavourings you're using, e.g. cinnamon, frozen berries.
2. Turn heat onto low-medium.
3. Stir constantly for about 4/5 minutes. Leave it a little runnier than you like it, as when you pour it into a bowl, it'll thicken slightly as it cools.
4. Top with fresh berries, fruit, shaved dark chocolate or dairy-free yoghurt.

Chocolate Overnight Oats
a wonderful, time-saving invention.

Ingredients

1/2 cup oats
1 cup milk
1 tsp cocoa powder

Recipe

1. Thoroughly whisk/blend the cocoa powder into the milk.
2. In a jam jar, Tupperware, plastic takeaway box, or whatever you've got, lay the oats.
3. Add the liquid mixture, and mix thoroughly with a fork/spoon, so that they're evenly coated.
4. Put a lid of some sort on them and find some space in the fridge. Leave them in until breakfast.
5. In the morning, chop up your fruit of choice and top. For example, banana and agave nectar/strawberries/raspberries/blueberries/apple and raisin.
6. Normally eaten cold.

Thick Pancakes
(fluffy, American style)

Ingredients

1/2 cup flour
1 tbsp sugar
1.5 tsp baking powder
Good pinch of salt
1 tsp cinnamon
1/2 cup milk
1 tbsp lemon juice

Recipe

1. In a measuring jug, combine the dry ingredients (flour, salt, sugar, baking powder, cinnamon).
2. Add the milk and mix thoroughly. Then, add the lemon juice and mix. Avoid mixing the milk and lemon juice in one or it may curdle your milk – pancakes ruined. Let the batter sit for 5 minutes before cooking it – you'll start to see lots of air bubbles pop through and this is a great sign.
3. Whilst the batter sits, start preparing your toppings: chop any fruit you're having.
4. When it comes to frying, melt a little bit of butter in a pan on a low heat.
5. Pour out some of the batter and let it spread. The first one is likely to remain quite flat, but don't despair: the first one is always a bad one.
6. After the first one, the pancakes should rise from the edges up and in slightly and you should see plenty of air bubbles across the surface of the pancake. When this happens, it's ready to be flipped.
7. Repeat until all the batter is gone.
8. Avoid stacking them straight onto a plate – as they cool, if they're stacked on top of each other they will go soggy.
9. Top tip: if you have time to spare, double the batter and make a big stack of pancakes. Freeze them once cooled and keep them for a rainy day. To eat them again, pop them in the toaster (not the microwave, they'll go soggy) and eat as normal.

Thin Pancakes
Crêpe style - this recipe must set before being used!

Ingredients

1 cup milk
5 tbsp dairy-free butter, melted
1 tbsp brown sugar
1 tbsp maple syrup
1 tbsp golden syrup
1 cup plain flour
1 tsp salt

Recipe

1. Melt the dairy-free butter.
2. Gently mix all ingredients together and store in the fridge overnight.
3. In the morning, heat some butter in a pan over a low heat.
4. Pour the batter on the pan and let the pancake cook all the way through, from one side.

Tofu Scramble

Ingredients

100g silken tofu (about 1/3 of a standard block)
2 cups/rather large amount of spinach (it withers! You need the iron!)
1/2 tsp garlic powder / 1 garlic clove, peeled and minced
1/2 tsp cumin
1/2 tsp turmeric
1/2 tsp salt
Sprinkle of pepper
1 tbsp olive oil

Recipe

1. Remove your tofu from the packaging. Squeeze the water out from the block against the side of sink (providing it's clean!) or just in between your hands over the drain.
2. Place your tofu on a chopping board. With a fork, mash the block gently, crumbling it into pieces. Chop a pepper here if you are using one.
3. In a pan, heat the oil and add the tofu (and the pepper, if you're using it).
4. Season by adding the garlic, cumin, turmeric, salt and pepper. Mix to ensure the tofu is evenly coated in oil and seasoning.
5. Add the spinach. When mixing, overturn the tofu on to the spinach. It will wilt under the heat of it all.
6. Cook for about 15 minutes. Colour changes here are not very helpful, as the tofu will stay yellow throughout, however, you will notice it should go a little golden brown/slightly crispy on the outside. However, if this happens too soon it could also be a sign that you're cooking on too high a heat.
7. Serve on toast, spread with hummus and a drizzle of ketchup. Drink a glass of orange juice/eat with a bowl of strawberries. Always pair iron dense meals with vitamin C to ensure the iron is absorbed effectively into your body.
"Mexican" version: cook with any leftover black beans and sweetcorn; serve with tomato salsa and mashed avocado. The Dorito mild salsa is vegan!

French Toast Sandwich

Ingredients

4 tsp plain flour
1.5 tsp cinnamon (and a sprinkle extra)
1 tbsp caster sugar
1 tbsp maple syrup
1/4 cup milk
Slices of bread
Dairy free butter, to fry in

Recipe

1. Combine all 5 ingredients (excluding bread) and mix/whisk until smooth.
2. Pour the liquid mixture into a wide rim, flat bowl or tray. Place a slice of bread in the mixture and let sit for a few seconds to absorb the liquid.
3. Using a spatula, flip the bread onto the other side, also allowing the liquid to absorb into the bread.
4. In a pan, over a medium heat, melt some butter.
5. Place the bread in the pan and let toast for about 45 seconds on each side/until golden brown.
6. Slice and enjoy, either by itself, with powdered sugar or with a scoop of (n)ice cream/chopped fruit/berries on top.
7. Top tip: make a peanut butter and banana sandwich and then soak the whole thing in the liquid before frying.

Nice Cream

Ingredients

3 bananas

Recipe

1. Slice the bananas into small slices and freeze them overnight.
2. In the morning, bring out the bananas and let them rest on the side for 10 minutes at room temperature.
3. Blend until a creamy consistency is reached. Occasionally scrape down the sides of the blender, if necessary. Add a tiny dash of milk to ease the process, if also necessary.
4. Top tip: plenty of supermarkets sell frozen fruits already, which are perfect for making things like nice cream or fruit sorbets. Blend anything with frozen bananas to make your nice cream flavoured: frozen berries or cocoa powder are always a winner.

Chia Seed Pudding

Ingredients

2/3 cup milk
2 tbsp chia seeds
1 tsp maple syrup (optional)

Recipe

1. In a jar, combine the milk and chia seeds. Mix gently but thoroughly.
2. Let sit on the side for 5 minutes. Some chia seeds with clump and sink to the bottom. With a fork, gently sift through these to separate them.
3. Once the chia seeds are evenly mixed throughout the milk, place a lid on the jar and keep in the fridge, either overnight or over the course of a working day.
4. Top with yoghurt, cinnamon, frozen fruit or a fruit puree.

Beetroot Smoothie Bowl
(with kiwi, chia seeds, desiccated coconut, shaved dark chocolate, frozen berries)

Ingredients

1 kiwi
1 small banana
1 tbsp desiccated coconut
1 small beetroot (steamed or boiled, then frozen)
1 tbsp chia seeds
1 tbsp shaved dark chocolate
1/2 cup frozen berries
Plant based milk of your choice (or yoghurt if you prefer thicker smoothies)
Trekking mix (optional; I buy a bag in Wilko for £1 and chuck it on all my smoothie bowls)

Recipe

1. Prepare: slice the kiwi (and peel it if you don't like the skin; I keep mine on).
2. Blend the milk/yoghurt and banana together. Add the beetroot and blend. Add 1/2 of half the cup of frozen berries. Save the other half for toppings.
3. Pour into a bowl and top with 1 line of chia seeds, 1 line of coconut, 1 line of sliced kiwi, the rest of berries, 1 line of shaved dark chocolate, 1 line of trekking mix.

Vegan Full English (with a meat substitute)

Ingredients

4 vegan sausages
1 avocado
Cherry tomatoes, on the vine (1 vine: 4 to 6 tomatoes)
Button mushrooms (garlic and balsamic vinegar)
Bread (fresh baguette preferable. Support your local bakery!)
Baked beans
1 cup spinach
1 pepper

Recipe

1. Preheat the oven to 170°C.
2. Line a baking tray with aluminium foil. Place the tomato vine on the tray and drizzle in olive oil. Place in the oven and leave for 5 to 7 minutes.
3. Next, add the sausages next to the tomatoes and cook according to instructions.
4. Make the mashed avocado. Cut the avocado in half and gently twist the two halves apart to separate them. Carefully use a knife to remove the stone. Spoon out the avocado flesh onto a chopping board. With a fork, mash to your desired consistency.
5. Slice your baguette.
6. Whilst the sausages and tomatoes cook, cook the mushrooms. In a pan, heat some oil and chuck in the mushrooms. Season with salt, pepper, balsamic vinegar and 2 minced garlic cloves. Sauté for approximately 7 minutes (until they've shrunk in size and turned a dark brown colour). Set aside once cooked.
7. Deseed and slice a pepper into strips. In the same pan used for the mushrooms, sauté the spinach and pepper until the spinach has wilted.
8. Chuck the beans in the microwave (not in the can) and toast your bread.
9. On a plate, arrange your feast!

Vegan Breakfast (without a meat substitute)

Ingredients

Sweet potato pancakes:

1 medium sweet potato
1 cup milk
1 tsp vegetable oil
1 cup flour
1.5 tsp baking powder
1 tsp cinnamon

Beetroot hummus:

1 portion of hummus (recipe in 'Sides') with 1 beetroot blended in

Balsamic garlic mushrooms – recipe in 'Sides'

Order of making

1. Garlic mushrooms
2. Sweet potato pancakes
3. Beetroot hummus

Recipe

Sweet potato pancakes:
1. Peel and cut the sweet potato into small chunks. Boil in water until soft.
2. Blend the sweet potato with the milk and vegetable oil.
3. Mix in the remaining pancake ingredients with a fork to form a smooth batter. Do not blend!
4. Heat some oil in a pan on a medium heat, spoon out some mixture and cook the pancakes. The pancakes will start to dry around the edges and thicken. Flip when ready!

Serving Suggestion
1. Add a generous dollop of hummus to a plate.
2. Stack the pancakes on top of each other, onto the hummus.
3. Place the mushrooms on top and any leftovers on the side.
4. Serve with a beetroot and orange side salad (recipe in 'Sides').

LUNCH

1. Green and Grape Salad
2. Mediterranean Pasta Salad
3. Sandwich/Pitta Bread fillings:
   a. Butter Bean and Avocado
   b. Mashed Avocado and Maple Fried Tofu
   c. Vegan BLT
   d. Red Pesto and BBQ Tofu
4. Wrap fillings:
   a. Broccoli and Apple
   b. Smashed Sweet Potato and Black Bean
   c. Fajitas
5. Apple and Beetroot Salad
6. Bean Pastry Pockets
7. Red Pesto Pasta with Black Olives and Spinach
8. Rainbow Buddha Bowl
9. Pasta e Fagioli
10. Lemon and Garlic Jackfruit (With Spinach and Rice)

Green and Grape Salad

Ingredients

1.5 cups chopped broccoli florets / 1/2 pack tender stem broccoli
1 white potato (medium)
1/2 cup peas
1/2 courgette
1/4 cup green beans (stood up in the cup)
1 tbsp olive oil
1/2 cup red grapes

Dressing (optional):

- Juice of 1 lemon
- A handful of fresh mint leaves or 2 cloves of garlic

Recipe

1. Scrub and chop the potato into chunks. Slice the courgette into circular slices. Chop the ends off the green beans, and wash and slice the grapes in half. Chop the florets off the broccoli head.
2. Boil the potatoes for 12-14 minutes, adding the peas, broccoli and green beans after the first 10 minutes.
3. In a separate pan, place the courgette with 1 tbsp olive oil and a sprinkle of salt and pepper. Sauté until soft and cooked. If you have a grill, you can also use it here to grill the courgette instead of lightly frying it!
4. Pick all the leaves off the stems of fresh mint. Chop very finely. Combine all ingredients for the sauce, if making it, and mix thoroughly.
5. Mix everything together in a bowl and serve.

Mediterranean Pasta Salad

Ingredients

2 cups pasta of your choice (farfalle/penne are the best, and this makes enough for today and tomorrow!)
Olive oil to your liking (I use 2 tbsp)
1/2 cup olives (preferably black)
1 can black eyed beans (in water)
1 cup cherry tomatoes
1/2 cup chopped cucumber
1 red onion
Juice of 1/2 lemon
Oregano
Salt and pepper

Recipe

1. Boil the pasta (for 10 to 12 minutes).
2. As it boils, prepare the vegetables; slice the olives in half (remove pits, if necessary). Chop the tomatoes into quarters if they're cherry, slice the cucumber, slice (not dice) the red onion thinly and rinse the black beans clean from the can.
3. When the pasta has finished cooking, drain it thoroughly.
4. Either in the saucepan or in a mixing bowl, combine the olives, onion, tomatoes and cucumber. Squeeze the lemon juice over the salad and season with salt, pepper and oregano to your liking.
5. Mix thoroughly!

Sandwich/Pitta Bread Fillings

Butter Bean and Avocado:
Ingredients

1/2 can butter beans (start with 1/2 can, add more later,
if necessary)
1 avocado
1/2 cup of fresh basil
Cucumber/spinach/tomatoes/all
Salt
Pepper
Juice of 1/2 a lemon
Leftover butter beans can be saved and used to thicken a soup, if necessary

Recipe

1. Drain and wash the white beans from the can.
2. In a bowl, mash the beans. If they're a little hard, chuck them in the microwave for 1 minute to soften.
3. Bunch the basil leaves together and slice finely.
4. Slice the avocado in half, remove the stone and peel the skin off/spoon the flesh out. Roughly mash with a fork.
5. Add the avocado to the beans and mix in the basil with the lemon juice, salt and pepper.
6. Serve in a sandwich with slices of cucumber for some crunch and tomato/spinach.

Mashed Avocado and Maple Fried Tofu

Ingredients

Cucumber/spinach leaves/both
1 avocado
100g firm (not silken, like for scrambles) tofu
3 tbsp maple syrup
1/4 cup low-sodium soy sauce
2 tsp ground ginger
Oil, of any kind for frying

Recipe

1. For the tofu; drain and slice it in 1/2 cm thick slices.
2. In a small bowl, whisk thoroughly the maple syrup, soy sauce and ginger.
3. You can either marinate the tofu the night before or just dip it in and pour the rest of the sauce over it as it cooks. Marinated gives better flavour but if you forgot to prep, just pour the sauce over the tofu in the pan (and make a note for next time).
4. In a pan over a low heat, heat the oil and gently lie the tofu in it. Cook until dark brown in colour. For a crispy outer coating, lay the slices in flour and nutritional yeast before frying.
5. Serve in a sandwich over mashed avocado and top with sliced cucumber/spinach leaves/both.

Vegan BLT

Ingredients

100g firm tofu
1/4 cup barbeque sauce
1 tsp smoked paprika
2 tbsp low sodium sauce
Oil for frying
Lettuce
1/2 large tomato
Vegan mayo/hummus

Recipe

1. Mix the barbeque sauce, soy sauce and smoked paprika together in a small bowl. Either marinate the tofu the night before or just cook it in the sauce.
2. In a pan, heat some oil and gently fry the tofu. Any remaining sauce can be added to the pan to cook it.
3. Serve on bread, either with hummus or vegan mayo, lettuce and sliced tomato.

Red Pesto and BBQ Tofu

Ingredients

4 slices silken tofu
1/4 cup BBQ sauce
2 tbsp low sodium soy sauce
1 tbsp oil
1/2 tbsp nutritional yeast
1 tsp black pepper
Red pesto (recipe in lunch section)
Cucumber
Fresh spinach
Sliced bread

Recipe

1. In a small pot, combine the BBQ sauce, soy sauce, nutritional yeast and black pepper.
2. In a pan, lay the slices of tofu in a very small drizzle of oil and gently fry each side for 1 minute.
3. Pour in the sauce you've just made and still on a low heat gently fry the slices for a further 3 minutes, or until a dark brown colour is reached.
4. Slice the cucumber.
5. In a sandwich, spread the red pesto on each slice of bread being used. Layer spinach leaves and cucumber in your desired proportions then place the sliced tofu on top. Seal the sandwich and slice in half.

Broccoli and Apple

Ingredients

1 cup chopped broccoli florets
1 large green apple
1/2 cup walnuts, chopped roughly
1/4 cup dried cranberries (optional)
1 large carrot, peeled and in ribbons
Vegan mayonnaise/cashew cream/hummus
Cucumber/tomatoes
Fresh spinach leaves/mixed rocket salad

Recipe

1. Chop off the small florets of broccoli. Steam or boil for 4 to 6 minutes.
2. Wash and slice the apple into halves and then in thin slices. Roughly chop the walnuts.
3. Peel the carrot and ribbon it (discard the peel and basically peel the carrot down to its core).
4. If you're making cashew cream, blend 1 cup of soaked cashews (or soak them in boiling water for 10 minutes, if you've forgotten to leave them overnight) with the juice of 1 lemon, 2 tbsp milk and 2 tbsp nutritional yeast. Let the broccoli cool completely, otherwise the cream will melt and drip/make the wrap soggy.
5. Refrigerate to solidify.
6. Open the wrap: lay a layer of spread (e.g. hummus/cashew cream), spinach/salad leaves, broccoli, apple, walnut.

Smashed Sweet Potato and Black Bean

Ingredients

2 sweet potatoes
1/2 can black beans
1 small tin sweetcorn
1 avocado
Plain yoghurt
Olive oil
Salt and pepper
Garlic powder
Chilli powder

Recipe

1. Preheat the oven to 180°C.
2. Peel the sweet potato and chop into small chunks. Place in a baking tray and drizzle in olive oil with a sprinkling of salt.
3. Roast them for 45 minutes. If you're short on time, dice the potatoes and boil the pieces for 10 minutes.
4. Rinse the black beans and sweetcorn under water, until it runs clear.
5. Halve, destone, peel and slice the avocado.
6. Remove the sweet potatoes from the oven.
7. Lay down a wrap.
8. Mash the sweet potato pieces onto a wrap with a fork. Lay the avocado slices up the middle of the wrap. Finish by adding the black bean mixture and wrap the wrap.
9. For a crunch, slowly crisp some onions in oil and add.

Fajitas

Ingredients

2 sweet peppers
1/2 box mushrooms
1 tbsp smoked paprika
1 onion
3 garlic cloves
1 tsp cumin
Salt and pepper

Recipe

1. Deseed and slice the peppers into strips. Slice the mushrooms. Chop the onion. Peel and mince the garlic cloves.
2. In a pan, gently heat some oil and add the onion, garlic, pepper and seasonings. Cook for 5 minutes.
3. Add the mushrooms.
4. Cook for a further 5 minutes.
5. Serve in a wrap with a pico de gallo (recipe in Turmeric Rice Burrito Bowl) and a dollop of plain yoghurt.

Apple and Beetroot Salad

Ingredients

1 cooked beetroot
1 green apple
1/4 cup walnuts
Mixed rocket leaf/fresh spinach
1/2 can green lentils / 1/3 cup dried, cooked

Recipe

1. Drain the green lentils from the can and rinse thoroughly until water runs clear. If boiling them, put them in a small pan and boil. This should take about 20 minutes.
2. Quarter, core and slice the apple into small chunks. Chop the beetroot into small pieces. Roughly chop the walnuts.
3. In a large bowl, combine the salad leaves, green lentils, apple, walnuts and beetroot.

Bean Pastry Pockets

Ingredient

1 sheet puff pastry
1/2 can baked beans
1 bag vegan cheese

Note: Mashed sweet potato and black beans with parsley also works well as a combination
Serve with a side salad

Recipe

1. Preheat the oven to 170°C.
2. Defrost the sheet of pastry and roll it out. Slice into 4 squares.
3. Drain the baked beans but keep the liquid in a separate bowl.
4. Using a teaspoon, spread a small amount of the baked bean liquid onto the centre of the pastry square. Spoon on some baked beans and sprinkle with dairy-free cheese.
5. Pull one corner of the square and fold it over in half, over to the opposite corner, making a triangle. Seal down the edges by pressing down the rim with a fork.
6. Brush some melted butter over the top.
7. Bake for 15 to 20 minutes.
8. Liquid will be EXTREMELY hot if leaking from the sides. Be careful not to burn yourself!

Red Pesto Pasta with Black Olives and Spinach

Ingredients

1 portion red pesto recipe below
1/2 cup black olives
2 cups fresh spinach
1.5 cups dried pasta

Recipe

1. Boil the pasta in salted water.
2. Drain the olives from their liquid and drain the pasta. Combine to the pasta with the red pesto sauce.
3. Add the spinach and stir, constantly overturning the pasta to ensure it all wilts adequately.

Homemade Red Pesto Sauce

Ingredients

2 large red peppers
3/4 cup sundried tomatoes
40g sachet pine nuts / 1/4 cup (optional)
Olive oil: 1/4 cup from the sundried tomato jar (drain the liquid into a small pot)
2 garlic cloves
1 tsp oregano/mixed green herbs
Sprinkle of chilli flakes

Recipe

1. Preheat the oven to 170°C.
2. Cut open the red peppers, remove the seeds and slice. Place on a baking tray and lightly drizzle in olive oil and oregano. Ensure everything is evenly coated before putting in the oven.
3. Place in the oven and roast for 40 minutes. In the last 10, add the pine nuts to the baking tray to toast them lightly. Remove once ready.
4. In a blender, combine all ingredients. Save the oil from the sundried tomato jar; you will need this!
5. Add 2 tbsp of the oil first. Blend and check the consistency of the sauce. If you like it chunky, leave it like this. If you like it a little runnier, add a tad more oil and keep going until you've made it how you like it.

Rainbow Buddha Bowl

Ingredients

1/2 cup brown rice
1 large tomato
1 large carrot
1 cup broccoli (about 5 florets, chopped smaller)
1 cup chopped red cabbage
1/2 can chickpeas
1 tsp chilli flakes
2 tsp cumin
2 tsp (olive) oil

Recipe

1. Wash and boil the brown rice (in 1.5 cups water). Boil for 12 minutes, steam for 8.
2. Whilst the rice boils, prepare your chickpeas. Drain and rinse them clean.
3. In a pan, coat the chickpeas in the cumin, chilli flakes and olive oil. Ensure everything is evenly coated. On a medium heat, cook the chickpeas, flipping them in the pan often. If you're not a fan of spicy foods, remove the chilli flakes from this recipe and replace the cumin with cinnamon.
4. Prepare the rest of your vegetables; peel the carrot into ribbons, chop the tomato into small chunks, snap the broccoli florets off the head and chop them into smaller pieces, and chop the red cabbage into pieces.
5. Steam the broccoli and cabbage in a pan of water or chuck it in with the chickpeas and cook until soft.
6. Once all cooked, arrange neatly in a bowl and enjoy!

Pasta e Fagioli

The bigger the saucepan the better. As a general rule of thumb, the size of the beans you use should be roughly the size of the pasta. Margheritine is the best pasta to use, as it's designed for pasta soups, but anything like conchiglie, farfalle, short rigatoni, dischi volanti will work!

Ingredients

1 onion
6 garlic cloves
2 sticks celery
1 large carrot
1 can butter beans
4 tbsp olive oil
1 can chopped tomatoes
3 cups water
1 stock cube
3/4 cup pasta
1 tsp dried thyme/mixed herbs
1 tsp salt and pepper each
3 tbsp nutritional yeast (optional – but get that B12 today somehow!)

Recipe

1. Prepare your vegetables; peel and dice the onion. Wash and chop the celery. Peel and chop the carrot into small pieces. Peel and mince the garlic.
2. In a pan, sauté the onion and garlic in the olive oil for about 3 to 4 minutes, until soft.
3. Drain the liquid from the beans into a measuring cup. Fill it up with water if there is room and transfer into a bigger jug. Add another 3 cups of boiling water into the jug. Dissolve the stock cube in it.
4. Add the vegetables and ensure they're evenly coated and mixed within the onion and garlic. Sauté for a further 3 minutes.
5. Add the chopped tomatoes, water and butter beans to the vegetables.
6. Bring to the boil.
7. Once boiling, add the pasta. Add the thyme, salt and pepper and nutritional yeast.
8. Stir often and cook for 20 minutes until the pasta is cooked.

Lemon and Garlic Jackfruit (with Spinach and Rice)

Ingredients

Rice:
1 tsp oil
1 slice lemon
1 large garlic clove (2 medium, crushed and chopped)
3/4 cup rice
Jackfruit:
1 can jackfruit pieces (in water)
1 tbsp olive oil
Juice of 2 lemons
6 garlic cloves, minced
1 tsp soy sauce
1 cup spinach

Recipe

1. To make the jackfruit marinade, combine the olive oil, lemon juice, garlic cloves and soy sauce together. Leave to soak for a few hours.
2. In a pan, pour the contents of the jackfruit in and cook on a medium heat until reduced. Once reduced, remove from the heat and add the spinach. Gently let wilt under the heat of the jackfruit. Sprinkle with salt and pepper, if desired.
3. Make the rice: fry the garlic in the oil for 2 minutes on a medium heat.
4. Add the rice and ensure that it is evenly coated in garlic and oil.
5. Add the rice and 1.5 cups water. Bring to the boil and once boiling, let simmer on a medium heat for 12 minutes with the slice of lemon.
6. After 12 minutes, steam for 8 by putting a plate on top of the saucepan, off the heat.

DINNER

1. Chilli Con Sausage Stew
2. Sweet Potato and Spinach Curry
3. Black Bean and Butternut Squash Curry
4. Mushroom and Kale 'Stew'
5. Sweet and Sour Tofu/Meat-free Chicken
6. Shepherd's Pie
7. Stuffed Peppers (with Sweet Potato Mash, Caramelised Onions and Sweetcorn)
8. Turmeric Rice Burrito Bowl
9. Spaghetti Bolognese
10. Jack's 'Cheesy' Vegetable Pasta
11. Mediterranean Tartlets
12. Jacket Sweet Potato, Hummus and Spinach
13. Pea and Walnut Pesto
14. Broccoli and Mushroom Noodles
15. Lemon and Crispy Smoked Tofu Pasta
16. Garlic and Sweet Chilli Stir Fry
17. Tomato Rice and Beans, Caramelised Onions and Tofu
18. Pea and Mushroom Risotto
19. Ratatouille
20. Lasagne

Chilli Con Sausage Stew

Ingredients

1 can red kidney beans in chilli sauce
1 can chopped tomatoes
4 of your favourite meat free sausages
1 onion
2 tbsp olive oil
Salt and pepper
1/2 cup rice

Recipe

1. Chop the onion. Heat in a pan with a generous drizzle of olive oil and sauté until aromatic and translucent.
2. Combine the chopped tomatoes, kidney beans and sausages over a medium/low heat. Stir well and let simmer gently for 15/20 minutes. In the meantime, prepare your rice.
3. Wash the rice. Place in a pan with 1.5 cups of water.
4. Boil the rice for 12 minutes, then take off the heat and let steam for 8 minutes by placing a plate over the top of the pan and leaving to rest.
5. Serve sausages over rice.

Sweet Potato and Spinach Curry

Ingredients

1 can chopped tomatoes
1 can coconut milk
1 sweet potato
1 can chickpeas (or 1/2 cup red lentils)
1 small bag of spinach / 2 stuffed cups
1 large onion
4 garlic cloves
2 tbsp tomato puree
1 tsp turmeric
1 tsp paprika
1 tsp chilli powder/flakes if you like spicy food!
1 tsp salt and pepper each
2 garlic cloves, minced
Fresh coriander
Rice to serve

Recipe

1. Prepare the vegetables. Peel and dice the onion, and garlic, peel and cut the sweet potato in chunks, and rinse the chickpeas from the liquid in their can.
2. In a pan, gently heat some oil and sauté the onion and garlic together. Two minutes in, add the turmeric, paprika, salt, pepper, chilli powder and tomato puree. Sauté for a further minute or two.
3. Add the coconut milk, chopped tomatoes, chickpeas/lentils and sweet potato. Bring to the boil and then let gently simmer for about 30 minutes. If using lentils, stir very often (otherwise they'll sink to the bottom and burn the pan).
4. Prepare your rice to accompany the curry here. Wash your rice, boil for 12 minutes, steam for 8.
5. Whilst the rice steams, add two generous handfuls of spinach into the curry pot. Stir the spinach into the curry, allowing it to wilt properly.
6. Serve the curry over the rice and enjoy.

Black Bean and Butternut Squash Curry

Ingredients

1 500g jar chilli sauce
1 can coconut milk
1 can black beans / 3/4 cup of peas, if you don't have any black beans (makes a pea and butternut squash curry)
2 tbsp olive oil
2 onions
4 garlic cloves, minced
2 tsp smoked paprika
2 tsp cinnamon
1 tsp nutmeg
2 tbsp tomato puree
1 small butternut squash

Recipe

1. Prepare your vegetables; peel and dice the onion, peel and mince the garlic, peel and chop the butternut squash into medium chunks, and drain the black beans from their can and rinse clean under water.
2. In a large saucepan, gently heat the oil, and sauté the onion and garlic together for 2 minutes.
3. Add the tomato puree, paprika, cinnamon and nutmeg. Cook for 1 more minute, ensuring the garlic and onion are evenly coated in spices.
4. Pour in the coconut milk and jar of chilli sauce. Mix well.
5. Add the butternut squash and black beans, and simmer for 40 minutes. Stir often to ensure that as it thickens it doesn't stick to the bottom of the pan.

Mushroom and Kale 'Stew'

Ingredients

1/2 box mushrooms
1.5 cups curly kale
1 celery stick
1/2 cup dried green lentils
1 can coconut milk
1 onion
2 tbsp olive oil
Salt and pepper
2 garlic cloves
2 tsp thyme
1 tbsp soy sauce
1 tbsp balsamic vinegar
1/4 cup apple juice/apple cider vinegar

Recipe

1. Prepare your vegetables. Slice the mushrooms (unless they're button mushrooms), dice the onion, mince the garlic, chop the celery and remove the curly kale leaves from the stalks.
2. In a pan, gently heat the oil and sauté the onion, garlic and celery together. Add the mushrooms and seasonings and cook for a further 2 minutes.
3. Add the coconut milk and green lentils. Bring this mixture to the boil and let simmer for 20 minutes. If the lentils are precooked (i.e. in a can already, rinse them from their liquid in the can and add them 5 minutes before the end).
4. Add the kale, soy sauce, balsamic vinegar and apple juice. Let simmer for a further 15/20 minutes on a medium to low heat.

Sweet and Sour Tofu/Meat-free Chicken

Ingredients

1 cup pineapple juice (normally enough in the tin but buy a little carton just in case)
1/4 cup apple cider vinegar
1/3 cup ketchup
1 tbsp cornflour
2 tbsp water
3 tbsp olive oil
4 garlic cloves
1 tsp chilli flakes
2 inches grated fresh ginger (use any leftover ginger to make ginger and lemon tea)
1 yellow/orange/red pepper; choose a colour
1 cup pineapple chunks
1 bag chicken pieces/1 small block firm tofu
1 tbsp soy sauce
Rice

Recipe

1. Prepare the fruit and vegetables.
2. Drain the liquid from the pineapple slices tin but keep the liquid, don't throw it away! Slice the pineapple and pepper of choice into chunks.
3. In a pan, combine all liquids (pineapple juice, apple cider vinegar, ketchup, water) and the cornflour. Whisk until the cornflour is completely dissolved in the liquid. Simmer on a medium heat, until a thick consistency is reached. Pour into a bowl and set aside.
4. In the same pan, combine the olive oil, garlic and ginger. Sauté for about 3 minutes.
5. Start preparing rice here. Boil some water, wash your rice and set it in a pan for 12 minutes, steam for 8 minutes.
6. To the pan with the garlic and ginger, add the pepper, pineapple, chicken pieces/tofu and cook for about 7 minutes.
7. Add the soy sauce and sweet and sour sauce back into the pan. Cook for a further 5 minutes.
8. Serve the sweet and sour chicken over the rice.

Shepherd's Pie

Ingredients

1 stick of celery
1 large carrot
1 large onion
Olive oil to sauté
4 large white potatoes
3 garlic cloves
1 cup meat-free mince or 1/2 cup green lentils
Salt
Nutritional yeast to top
Dairy-free butter, 1/4 cup
Pepper
1/4 cup vegetable gravy granules
2 tbsp olive oil

Recipe

1. Preheat the oven to 170°C.
2. Prepare your vegetables. Wash and slice the celery. Peel and slice the carrot into circular slices (bigger slices can be cut in half). Peel and dice the onion. Peel and chop the potatoes into chunks. Peel and mince the garlic.
3. Place the potato chunks in water and leave to boil for 10 minutes.
4. In a pan, gently heat some oil and fry the onion and garlic until soft.
5. If using green lentils, wash and set to boil here. Boil for 15 minutes.
6. Add the carrots and celery to the onion and garlic. Sauté for a further 5 minutes.
7. Add in the mince/lentils and cook for 10/15 minutes, according to the packet (they all vary slightly), on a medium heat.
8. Make the gravy by mixing the granules with water, according to the packaging instructions. Make it more on the thin side, as it'll thicken when it cooks in the oven.
9. Add the gravy to the saucepan cooking the meat-free mince/lentils. Cook for a further 3 minutes on a low heat, mixing completely.
10. Drain the potatoes and mash them. Add dairy-free butter and milk for extra creamy mash.
11. In an ovenproof dish, lay the mince mixture.
12. Layer the mash on top, covering the whole dish.
13. Evenly spread some butter over the top and generously cover in nutritional yeast. Cook for 25 minutes in the oven.

Stuffed Peppers
(with sweet potato mash, caramelised onions and sweetcorn)

Ingredients

2 peppers, colours of your choice
1 medium sweet potato
1 small tin of sweetcorn
1 white onion and 1 red, peeled and sliced (not diced)
Salt
Pepper
Olive oil and 3 tbsp brown sugar
Paprika
Serve with a simple side salad of mixed rocket, chopped cherry tomatoes and a balsamic vinegar (glaze) / green beans / you can roast some vegetables at the same time as the peppers, e.g. carrots/parsnips.

Recipe

1. Preheat the oven to 170°C.
2. Slice the tops off the peppers and remove the insides. Place on a baking tray, drizzle some olive oil and sprinkle a little salt over the top. Place in the oven for 20 minutes.
3. Peel and chop the sweet potato. Boil for about 15 minutes/until it slides off a knife.
4. As it boils, in a pan, gently heat some oil and cook the onions for 3 minutes. Add the brown sugar and on a low heat, stir constantly to soften (it takes about 6 to 9 minutes).
5. Mash the sweet potatoes until smooth, adding salt and pepper here. Drain the corn from its liquid in the can and add to the mashed sweet potato. Add the onions and paprika. Stir well, mixing all ingredients well.
6. Remove the peppers from the oven and stuff them with the sweet potato mixture.
7. Place back in the oven for a further 15 minutes.
8. Prepare the salad; in a bowl, combine some mixed leaves, chopped cherry tomatoes and drizzle in a balsamic glaze.

Turmeric Rice Burrito Bowl

Ingredients

Pico de Gallo:
1 tin chopped tomatoes
1 red onion
Sprinkle of salt and pepper
1 tbsp olive oil
1/4 cup fresh parsley

Cashew cream drizzle:
3/4 cup of soaked cashews (overnight)
1 tbsp nutritional yeast
1/2 cup milk
Salt and pepper

Burrito bowl:
1/2 cup rice
2 tsp turmeric
1/2 can black beans
1 small tin corn
1/2 cucumber
1 pepper of your colour choice

Recipe

Rice:

1. Wash and boil the rice (cook for 12 minutes, steam for 8). Boil with 1.5 cups of water (with a little extra if necessary, as the turmeric can be quite drying). Cook with 1 tsp of turmeric.

Pico de Gallo:

2. Dice the red onion finely.
3. Chop the parsley.
4. Combine all ingredients and season generously with olive oil, salt and pepper.

Cashew cream drizzle:

5. Blend all ingredients for the drizzle. If you forgot to soak them during the day/overnight, leave them for 10 minutes in freshly boiled water.

Vegetables:

6. Deseed and chop the pepper and dice the cucumber.
7. Drain the black beans and sweetcorn from their cans, wash thoroughly in a sieve and mix together.

Putting the bowl together:

8. Arrange all components in a bowl in strips; turmeric rice, Pico de Gallo, chopped pepper and cucumber, black beans and drizzle with the cashew cream.

Spaghetti Bolognese

Ingredients

Meat free mince (1.5 cups) / 1/2 cup green lentils, cooked
1 can chopped tomatoes
1 carrot
1 onion
3 garlic cloves, minced
Spaghetti
Salt and pepper
Vegan cheese (optional)

Recipe

1. If you've got a pasta ladle with one single hole in the middle, the hole is the typical portion size for dried spaghetti. You can use it to measure out how much to cook.
2. Prepare your vegetables; peel and slice the carrot in half, down the middle vertically. Hold the sides together and slice further, horizontally all along the carrot. Peel and dice the onion and peel and mince the garlic cloves.
3. In a pan, heat some oil and sauté the onion, garlic and carrot.
4. In a separate pot of boiling water, salt it and lay in the spaghetti. Push the ends in gently as they soften.
5. Using the same pan as the onion/garlic, add the mince/cooked lentils. Sauté until soft and translucent.
6. Pour in the chopped tomatoes. Let simmer on a medium heat for 15 minutes.
7. Serve over the spaghetti and sprinkle with vegan cheese.
8. Top tip: use any leftover Bolognese mix to stuff a pepper and roast it!

Jack's 'Cheesy' Vegetable Pasta

In my final year student house, my housemate Jack loved cheese, like so many of us. This recipe was developed to satisfy those cravings and it definitely does the job! We use broccoli, spinach and black olives but you can use any vegetables you like.

Ingredients

1.5 cups pasta
1/4 of a broccoli
1/2 cup black olives, sliced
1 cup spinach
1 onion
1 tbsp mixed herbs (e.g. oregano, thyme, basil etc)
3 garlic cloves
2 tbsp olive oil
1.25 cups milk
1.5 tbsp cornflour
1/4 cup nutritional yeast (add more to your taste if desired)
Juice of 1/2 a lemon

Recipe

1. Prepare the vegetables. Chop the broccoli florets off, slice the black olives, peel and dice the onion and peel and mince the garlic.
2. Blend the ingredients to make the 'cheese' sauce together, until smooth: combine the milk, nutritional yeast, cornflour and lemon juice. Season with salt and pepper if desired.
3. In a pan, start boiling the pasta.
4. In a separate pan, sauté the onion, garlic and mixed herbs in the olive oil until translucent and aromatic.
5. Add the broccoli and cook for 3 minutes.
6. Add the sauce and on a low heat reduce until thick.
7. Drain the pasta.
8. Add the olives, spinach and pasta and thoroughly mix everything together. Serve once the spinach has wilted.

Mediterranean Tartlets

Ingredients

1 bag frozen Mediterranean vegetables (or a fresh courgette, aubergine, cherry tomatoes, red onion and basil)
1/4 cup pitted olives
3 tbsp tomato purée
1 tsp cumin
1 tsp dried basil
Salt and pepper
1 roll puff pastry
1 red onion

- Tomato puree
- Red onion slice
- Mixed veg

Recipe

1. Preheat the oven to 175°C.
2. Defrost the puff pastry and roll it out when ready. Be careful not to crack it.
3. Prepare your vegetables; peel and slice the red onion into rings Slice the olives if they're whole. If using fresh veg, cut into thin slices and small chunks.
4. In a small side bowl, mix together the tomato purée and seasonings. Add a drizzle of olive oil, if too thick.
5. Cut the pastry into 6 squares (laying it in a rectangle in front of you, cut 1 line horizontally and then 3 cuts vertically).
6. In the centre of each square, using a teaspoon, place a dollop of tomato purée mixture in the centre and spread outwards using the back of the spoon, about 1/2 cm from the edge all the way around.
7. Place a cross section of onion in the middle and arrange some mixed vegetables on top. Continue until all tartlets are ready.
8. I don't know how to describe the final decoration method I use so I have a diagram. The red lines indicate where to slice.
9. Where the corners meet (top left and bottom right), lift the corner and fold it in towards the centre of the tartlet, gently pulling it in to the middle.
10. Bake in the oven for 30 minutes on a greaseproof papered tray.
11. Serving suggestions: paprika potatoes and mixed leaf salad.

Jacket Sweet Potato, Hummus and Spinach

(I once made this on a night I was feeling very tired and a friend of mine came to visit. He tried it and gave the rest of his house the idea and now they all regularly make it). Extremely simple recipe, but honestly delicious.

Ingredients

1 large baking sweet potato
Two large handfuls of fresh spinach
Hummus of any flavour (I prefer plain here)

Recipe

1. Preheat the oven to 180°C.
2. Grab the sweet potato, and using a fork, poke some holes all over it. Slice it almost right through down the middle to the bottom, but not quite all the way through. Drizzle olive oil in the crack and outside on the skin (this gets messy!). Place on some aluminium foil and bring the sides of the foil up to wrap the potato. Roll the top of the foil down to seal the potato in.
3. Roast it for 50 minutes.
4. Fill your time somehow, as there's literally nothing left to do now until they're done. Check out Cooking Top Tip #12 for ideas on how to fill your time as you wait!
5. Serve on a plate with a generous dollop of hummus down the middle and a heavy load of fresh spinach leaves on top.

Pea and Walnut Pesto

Ingredients

1.5 cups frozen peas
3/4 cup walnuts
5 mint stalks (about 30 leaves)
1/2 tsp salt
Scrunch of pepper
Juice of 1/2 large lemon
4 tbsp olive oil
2 garlic cloves

Method

1. Boil your peas for 3 minutes
2. Before blending everything together, let the peas cool slightly.
3. Add all ingredients to a blender!
4. Serve over pasta with chopped cherry tomatoes or use as a sandwich spread.

Broccoli and Mushroom Noodles

Ingredients

2 cloves fresh garlic
1 pack of cooked, thick udon noodles
1/2 head of broccoli
1.5 cups button mushrooms
2 tbsp soy sauce
1 stock cube
Plum and hoisin sauce (optional)
Crushed cashews (I stick a handful in a plastic bag and whack them with a rolling pin)

Recipe

1. Prepare the vegetables; remove the florets of broccoli from the head and slice the garlic thinly.
2. In a saucepan, boil the broccoli for 2 minutes with the stock cube. When boiled, save 1/4 cup of stock for later.
3. In a pan, fry the cloves of garlic in some oil and 1 tbsp soy sauce.
4. Add the broccoli and mushrooms. Cook for 1 minute.
5. Add the noodles. Make sure everything is evenly coated and well mixed in each other.
6. Add the stock to help cook the noodles. Let simmer for 5 minutes.
7. Once the stock has evaporated, add the plum sauce here, if you're using it.
8. Serve with crushed cashews over the top.

Note: If you're using dried noodles, cook the noodles in the broccoli stock broth with 2 tbsp soy sauce. Add broccoli and can also add chunks of tofu for extra protein.

Lemon and Crispy Smoked Tofu Pasta

Ingredients

200g smoked tofu
1 tbsp nutritional yeast
2.5 tsp cornstarch
2 cups milk
1 large lemon (zest and all its juice, between 1/3 and 1/2 cup, depending on how strong you want the sauce to taste of lemon)
Pinch of salt
2 cups dried pasta
1 tbsp olive oil
Fresh parsley (optional)

Recipe

1. Cut the tofu into cubes. In a bowl, combine 1/2 tsp cornstarch with 1 tbsp nutritional yeast and place all the tofu cubes in this bowl. Using a spoon, toss them around to coat them evenly.
2. Thoroughly whisk 2 tsp cornstarch into the milk. If any lumps remain, give it a quick blend.
3. In a pan, combine the milk and cornstarch mixture with all the lemon zest and a pinch of salt. Bring to a simmer and whisk until thick. Pour into a glass and set aside.
4. Give your pan a quick clean under the tap. Bring it back to the hob and heat the olive oil. Add the tofu cubes (with any leftover nutritional yeast/cornstarch dust) and fry until they turn crispy and dark brown on the outside. If you like your tofu extra crispy, add more olive oil and fry them for even longer.
5. Salt your pasta water and set your pasta to boil.
6. Once your pasta has finished boiling, drain all the water out. Add your creamy sauce back into the pan and on a low heat, stir in the lemon juice. Sauces thicken slightly as they cool so reduce it until it's a little runnier than your desired consistency.
7. Mix in the tofu cubes and sprinkle with some fresh parsley to serve.

Garlic and Sweet Chilli Stir Fry

Ingredients

6 cloves garlic
1 large handful mangetout
1 sachet sweet chilli sauce (or make it from the Sweet and Sour
Tofu recipe)
1/2 a broccoli
4 baby corns
1 sweet pepper (any colour)
100g tofu pieces (optional)
2 tbsp vegetable oil

Recipe

1. Prepare the vegetables; deseed and chop the pepper into small pieces, remove the broccoli florets from the head, chop the baby corn into small pieces and peel and mince the garlic.
2. Boil/steam the broccoli; however you prefer it.
3. In a wok/large pan, gently heat the oil on a low heat and add the minced garlic. Sauté for 3 minutes. Add the chopped tofu and sauté on a medium heat for a further 8-10 minutes, until crispy.
4. Add the mangetout, cooked/steamed broccoli, baby corns and pepper here. Sauté for 2 minutes before adding the sweet chilli sauce.
5. Cook for a further 5 minutes.

Tomato Rice and Beans, Caramelised Onions and Tofu

(It is also an amazing burrito filling. Any leftovers I have I save for lunch the following day in a wrap!)

Ingredients

1/2 cup rice
1 vegetable stock cube
2 tbsp tomato purée
Sprinkle of salt and pepper
1/2 can black/kidney beans (either work well)
1 large onion
1 tsp brown sugar
1 small tin sweetcorn
1 cup chopped tofu/meat-free pieces

Recipe

1. Prepare vegetables; drain the sweetcorn and the black beans from the can, peel and chop the onion and chop the tofu into chunks.
2. Rinse the rice under cold water. In a pan, gently fry the rice in 1 tbsp olive oil. Ensure all the rice is evenly coated in oil.
3. Boil 1.5 cups water and measure out into a jug. Dissolve the stock cube and tomato purée in the water.
4. Pour the water over the rice. Reduce the heat once boiling and simmer for 10 minutes. After 10 minutes, mix in the black beans and simmer for a further 2 minutes.
5. In a pan, gently heat some oil with the brown sugar. Chuck in the chopped onion and tofu.
6. Add the corn and cook all together (should take around 10 minutes).
7. Steam the rice for 8 minutes, when ready.
8. Serve both together in a bowl or in a wrap/burrito.

Pea and Mushroom Risotto

(Mushrooms can also be replaced with asparagus, when in season). It's a good way to use any leftover white wine from pre's the night before!

Ingredients

1 cup risotto/arborio rice
1 tbsp olive oil
4 cups water (with 1 stock cube dissolved in)
1/3 cup white wine/apple cider vinegar
1 cup peas
1.5 cups chopped mushrooms (roughly 200g)
1 onion
4 cloves garlic
1 tsp thyme
3 tbsp nutritional yeast
Sprinkle of salt and pepper

Recipe

1. Peel and chop the onion. Peel and mince the garlic cloves. Set aside.
2. Prepare the stock by combining 4 cups of boiled water with a stock cube and dissolving it well. Set aside.
3. In a pan, gently heat the olive oil and sauté the onion and garlic for a few minutes, until translucent and soft.
4. Add the mushrooms and cook for 5 minutes, stirring often. Sprinkle with salt and pepper.
5. Add the rice and mix everything well.
6. Add the wine/apple cider vinegar. Simmer off the alcohol until it's reduced almost completely.
7. Now start by adding 1 cup of water. Wait until the majority of this water has been absorbed before adding the next.
8. Add 1/2 cup of water at a time, waiting for nearly all of it to absorb before adding another 1/2 cup.
9. Keep going, adding 1/2 cups of stock. Just before adding the last 1/2 cup, add the nutritional yeast, the thyme and the peas.
10. Add the final 1/2 cup of water. Remove from heat when a thick sauce surrounds the risotto but is not fully absorbed.
11. Serve with a slice of fresh lemon (squeeze in and stir before eating)!

Ratatouille

Ingredients

1 large courgette
1 aubergine
2 large tomatoes
1 red pepper
8 cloves garlic
1 tin of chopped tomatoes
1 small onion
2 tbsp olive oil
1/2 tsp chilli flakes (optional)

Recipe

1. Prepare your vegetables; slice everything into equal sized slices. Peel and mince the garlic. Peel and dice the onion. Deseed and chop the pepper into small chunks.
2. Preheat the oven to 140°C.
3. In a saucepan, sauté the onion and garlic for a couple minutes, until soft and translucent.
4. Add the tin of chopped tomatoes and pepper, and simmer until reduced (15/20 minutes).
5. Lay the tomato base in a small baking tin or tray. Layer the courgette, aubergine and tomato in an alternating fashion on top.
6. Cover with foil and bake in the oven for 2.5 hours.

Lasagne

Great for a busy week ahead – you can cook in bulk and freeze it!

Ingredients

Lasagne:
1/3 cup green lentils
1 small aubergine
1 pepper (any colour)
1 small carrot
1 large onion
1 garlic bulb (8 or 9 cloves)
1.5 cups sliced mushrooms
1.5 cups finely chopped kale/spinach
2 tins chopped tomatoes
3 tbsp olive oil
1 tbsp oregano/mixed herbs
9 lasagne sheets

Bechamel sauce:
1 tbsp nutritional yeast
2 cups milk
3 tbsp olive oil
2 tbsp flour
Salt and pepper

Recipe

Lasagne filling
1. Set the lentils to boil, if they're not coming from a can.
2. Prepare the vegetables: finely dice the onion, aubergine, pepper and carrot, peeling where necessary. Slice the mushrooms. Peel and mince the garlic.
3. Preheat the oven to 180°C.
4. In a large pan, heat the oil and sauté the onion and garlic.
5. Add the aubergine, pepper, carrot, mushrooms and herbs. Mix until all is covered in oil and well mixed through.
6. Drain and add the lentils, once boiled, followed by the chopped tomatoes and greens. Let simmer for about 20 minutes, until reduced.

Bechamel sauce:
1. In a pan, gently heat the oil and add the flour to form a paste.
2. Add the milk and nutritional yeast, bit by bit. Whisk in thoroughly and cook until a thick and smooth sauce forms.

Lasagne sheets:
1. Boil each lasagne sheet individually and set aside once cooked.

Assembling the lasagne:
1. In an ovenproof dish, lay 3 lasagne sheets on the bottom, top with filling and then drizzle some sauce on top. Repeat 2 more layers, or until all filling, sheets and sauce has been used.
2. Sprinkle the top with nutritional yeast and bake in the oven for 45 minutes.
16. Bake in the oven for 45 minutes.

SOUPS

1. White: Chickpea
2. Red: Red Pepper and Tomato
3. Orange: Carrot and Ginger
4. Green: Pea and Mint
5. Pink: Kidney Bean

White: Chickpea

Ingredients

1 can chickpeas
1 white potato, medium
1/2 tsp rosemary or thyme
1 onion
2 garlic cloves
2.5 cups water
Olive oil

Recipe

1. Peel and chop the onion and garlic. Drain the chickpeas from their can and rinse clean. Peel and chop the potato.
2. In a pan, sauté the onion and garlic in some olive oil.
3. After 4/5 minutes, add the potato. Cook for 5 minutes.
4. Add remaining ingredients and simmer for 20 minutes.
5. Blend when ready (cool completely FIRST before blending, otherwise the blender will explode under the pressure of the heat).

Red: Red Pepper and Tomato

Ingredients

1 can chopped tomatoes
1 red pepper
1 onion
Olive oil
2 cups of water

Recipe

1. Peel and finely chop the onion. Deseed and chop the pepper.
2. Gently heat some oil and sauté the onion.
3. After 4/5 minutes, add all remaining ingredients and simmer over a medium/low heat for 20 minutes, stirring often.
4. Blend when ready (cool completely FIRST before blending, otherwise the blender will explode under the pressure of the heat).

Orange: Carrot and Ginger

Ingredients

5 to 6 carrots
2 inches fresh ginger, minced
5 garlic cloves
1 vegetable stock cube
3 tbsp olive oil
2 cups water
1 small sweet potato/ 1/2 large
1 onion

Recipe

1. Peel, crush and chop the garlic cloves. Peel and slice the carrots and onion. Peel and chop the sweet potato.
2. In a saucepan, gently heat some oil and sauté the onion and garlic. After 3 to 4 minutes, add the carrots and ginger.
3. Boil two cups of water. Dissolve the stock cube in it and add to the carrots/onions/garlic.
4. Add the sweet potato.
5. Boil for 25 minutes.
6. Blend when ready (cool completely FIRST before blending, otherwise the blender will explode under the pressure of the heat).
7. Once in the fridge, I always leave a thin slice of ginger in the soup to infuse deeper (offers a richer flavour and I love ginger).

Green: Pea and Mint

Ingredients

1.5 cup peas
1 white potato, medium
1 garlic clove
1 small onion
1 tbsp olive oil
3 sprigs fresh mint
2 cups water

Recipe

1. Peel and finely chop the onion. Peel and chop the potato into chunks.
2. Gently heat the olive oil in a pan and over a low heat, sauté the onion with a few mint leaves.
3. Add the peas and potato. Sauté for about 2/3 minutes.
4. Add the water and bring to the boil.
5. Remove the leaves from the mint stalks. Add in half the mint as the soup cooks.
6. Cook for 20 minutes. Blend when ready, with the remaining mint leaves (cool completely FIRST before blending, otherwise the blender will explode under the pressure of the heat).

Pink: Kidney Bean

Ingredients

1 can kidney beans
1 onion (red or brown, either works well)
1 white potato, medium
1 tbsp olive oil
1 tsp salt
Sprinkle of pepper

Recipe

1. Prepare the vegetables: peel and dice the onion and peel and chop the potato into pieces. Set 2 cups of water to boil.
2. Over a medium heat, sauté the onion in the oil until soft.
3. Add the potato and sauté for a further 2 minutes.
4. Add the water, kidney beans, salt and pepper. Simmer for 15 minutes with a lid on.
5. Blend when ready (cool completely FIRST before blending, otherwise the blender will explode under the pressure of the heat).

SIDES

1. Balsamic Vinegar Roasted Mushrooms
2. Sticky Pulled Carrots
3. Steamed Rice
4. Roast Dinner Stuffing
5. Paprika Roasted Potatoes
6. Sweet Potato and Rosemary/Thyme Wedges
7. Boil and Bake Wedges
8. Beetroot and Orange Salad
9. White Bean and Avocado Side Salad
10. Hummus

Balsamic Vinegar Roasted Mushrooms

Ingredients

1 box button mushrooms
2 tbsp olive oil
2 tbsp balsamic vinegar
1 tbsp golden syrup
4 or 5 garlic cloves
1/2 tbsp thyme
Salt and pepper

Recipe

1. Preheat the oven to 180°C.
2. Prepare the vegetables; wash the mushrooms gently, and peel and mince the garlic.
3. In a small bowl, whisk together the olive oil, balsamic vinegar, garlic, golden syrup and thyme with a fork.
4. Arrange the mushrooms on a baking tray and coat in the sauce.
5. Place in the oven and roast for 20 minutes.
6. Toss them in their tray.
7. Roast for a further 20 minutes.
8. Garnish with chopped fresh spring onions (optional).

Sticky Pulled Carrots

Ingredients

3 large carrots
1 red onion
1 tbsp olive oil
Salt and pepper
1/2cup ketchup
1/4 cup BBQ sauce (optional)
2 tbsp apple cider vinegar
1/2 tsp cumin
1 tsp paprika

Recipe

1. Preheat the oven to 200°C.
2. Line a baking tray with tin foil/greaseproof paper.
3. Prepare the vegetables; peel and thickly grate the carrots. Peel and thinly slice the red onion.
4. Make the sauce by mixing the ketchup, BBQ sauce, apple cider vinegar, cumin and paprika together.
5. Place the carrots on a baking tray and cover with the sauce.
6. Cover with foil and roast for 20 minutes.
7. Remove the foil and roast for a further 10 minutes.

Steamed Rice

Ingredients

1/2 cup of rice
1.5 cups water
2 garlic cloves
1.5 tbsp olive oil

Recipe

1. Thoroughly wash the rice. Peel and slice the garlic.
2. In a pan, gently heat the oil and garlic. Sauté for 1 minute.
3. Add the rice and make sure it's completely coated in oil.
4. Add the water; bring to the boil, lower the heat and let simmer for 12 minutes without a lid.
5. Take off the heat and stir. Put a lid/plate on the pan. Let steam for 8 minutes.

Roast Dinner Stuffing

Ingredients

1/3 cup dairy-free butter
1/3 pack fresh sage
1 red apple
1 pear
1 stick celery
3/4 cup milk
Salt and pepper
1 bag croutons/2 cups of stale bread cut into chunks
1/2 cup walnuts

Recipe

1. Preheat the oven to 160°C.
2. Prepare the fruit and vegetables; peel, core and chop the apple into small pieces, core and dice the pear, wash and slice the celery, slice the sage and roughly chop the walnuts.
3. Melt the butter, and in a mixing bowl, combine the butter, croutons and milk. Let sit for 10 minutes (make sure the croutons are well coated in the mixture, add a little more milk if necessary).
4. Add the remaining ingredients and roast in a covered dish/ovenproof dish covered in aluminium foil for 30 minutes. If you notice the croutons are going dry (which they shouldn't as they're covered), add a little more milk and butter. Ensure it's cooked with a lid. If you don't have one, cover in tin foil.
5. Serve alongside a roast!

Paprika Roasted Potatoes

Ingredients

4 white potatoes
Paprika
Olive oil

Recipe

1. Preheat the oven to 170°C.
2. Prepare the potatoes; peel and cut them into small chunks.
3. Lay in a baking tray, all on a single layer and fill it with water, 3/4 of the way up the potatoes.
4. Douse generously in olive oil on top of the water.
5. Cover the top of the potatoes completely in paprika.
6. Roast for 40 minutes.

Sweet Potato and Rosemary/Thyme Wedges

Ingredients

Rosemary/thyme seasoning
2 sweet potatoes
Salt and pepper
Olive oil
Cayenne pepper (optional)

Recipe

1. Preheat the oven to 180°C.
2. Wash and slice the sweet potatoes into wedges.
3. Coat in olive oil and seasoning.
4. Roast for 30 minutes.

Boil and Bake Wedges

Ingredients

3 medium potatoes (not new size but not jacket size)
Olive oil
Salt and pepper
Smoked paprika
Garlic powder/granules
Piri Piri seasoning/chilli flakes (optional)

Recipe

1. Preheat the oven to 190°C.
2. Wash the potatoes well and slice them into wedges/thick, chunky sticks.
3. Place in a pan of boiling water for 7 minutes.
4. Transfer them onto a foil-lined baking tray and cover in olive oil and all remaining seasonings.
5. Mix all ingredients together and ensure the potatoes are evenly coated in everything.
6. Bake in the oven for 15 minutes, toss onto the other side and bake for a further 15 minutes.
7. Remove from the oven or until golden and slightly crispy around the edges of the slices.

Beetroot and Orange Salad

Ingredients

1 cooked beetroot
1 orange

Recipe

1. Chop the beetroot into chunks.
2. Peel and slice the orange horizontally through the segments. Chop further into small pieces.
3. Combine the two together in a bowl.

White Bean and Avocado Side Salad

Ingredients

1 can drained butter beans
1 cup freshly chopped tomatoes
2 spring onions
1/2 cup sliced olives
1 ripe avocado
Juice of 1/2 lemon
Sprinkle of salt and pepper

Recipe

1. Drain the beans from their liquid and wash well.
2. Wash and chop the cherry tomatoes into quarters/eighths (quarter the tomato and then halve each quarter).
3. Slice the spring onions and olives.
4. Slice the avocado in half, destone and remove the flesh. Chop into small chunks.
5. In a mixing bowl, combine all ingredients and season with salt and pepper and lemon juice.

Hummus

Ingredients

1 can chickpeas
2 garlic cloves
The juice of 1 lemon
1/4 cup olive oil
1/2 tsp salt
2 tsp cumin
2 tbsp water
2 tbsp tahini (optional)
3 sundried tomatoes (optional, to make flavoured hummus)
1/2 tsp chilli flakes (optional)

Recipe

1. Rinse the chickpeas clean. Peel the garlic clove and juice the lemon.
2. Blend all ingredients, until smooth.

DESSERTS

1. Brownies
2. Chocolate Tofu Pudding
3. Crumble
4. Grilled Cinnamon Pineapple Slices and Ice Cream
5. Banana Muffins

Brownies

Ingredients

2 cups flour
1 cup plant-based milk
1 cup brown sugar
1 cup white sugar
1 tsp salt
1 tbsp vanilla
1 tbsp maple syrup
3/4 cup cocoa powder
1/2 cup vegetable oil
1 tbsp baking powder
1 tsp baking soda

Recipe

1. Preheat the oven to 170°C.
2. In a pan, over a low heat, combine 1 cup of flour and the 1 cup of milk. Whisk constantly (with a fork or a whisk), until it forms a thick goo and no lumps are present. If you can feel it coagulate in the pan, it's burnt. The mixture must be smooth and lump free.
3. Set aside and cool.
4. In a mixing bowl, combine the sugar, vanilla, cocoa powder and vegetable oil.
5. Whisk thoroughly.
6. Add the flour-milk mix.
7. Whisk thoroughly.
8. Add the remaining cup of flour and baking powder.
9. Bake for 40/45 minutes.

Chocolate Tofu Pudding

(If you have any leftover ripe avocados you can use them here. Pudding won't taste of avocado at all, but it adds a creamier texture)

Ingredients

280g cubed silken tofu
2 tbsp cocoa powder (can be increased, depending on your personal taste)
1/4 cup milk
3 tbsp maple syrup
Half a ripe avocado (optional)

Recipe

1. Prepare the avocado (if using it); peel and chop the avocado into pieces.
2. In a blender, combine all ingredients and blend until smooth.
3. Stir well and re-blend to ensure no pockets of cocoa powder were missed. Taste as you go and add more cocoa powder if you want a stronger taste.
4. Pour into pots and chill. Serve with grated chocolate or fresh red berries.

Crumble

(Recipe is for apple, but any fruit can be used)

Ingredients

2 cups peeled, chopped fruit, e.g. 3 apples
1/4 cup brown sugar
1 tsp cinnamon
1 tbsp maple syrup/agave nectar/golden syrup
1/4 cup flour
1 cup (rolled) oats
1/3 cup butter
1/4 cup white sugar
1 tbsp cinnamon

Recipe

1. Preheat the oven to 180°C.
2. Prepare your fruit; peel, deseed and chop your fruit of choice into chunks.
3. In a saucepan, cook the fruit on a low heat with the brown sugar, cinnamon and maple syrup/agave nectar.
4. In a mixing bowl, combine the sugar, flour, oats and cinnamon. Mix well.
5. Add the butter and with your fingers, pass it through your fingertips gently until a crumble consistency is reached.
6. Pour the apple mixture into an ovenproof dish. Ensure that the fruit fills to the sides of the dish with at least one layer of fruit in it.
7. Cover the fruit in the dish with the crumble mixture, sprinkling a small amount of brown sugar and cinnamon on top.
8. Cook for 30 minutes.
9. Serve with dairy-free custard, if desired.

Grilled Cinnamon Pineapple Slices and Ice Cream

Ingredients

4 pineapple slices
1 tbsp brown sugar
1/2 tsp ground cinnamon
Dairy free ice cream/nice cream

Recipe

1. Drain the pineapple slices from their juice completely.
2. In a small bowl/glass, mix the cinnamon and brown sugar together. Place on a small plate and gently shake from side to side to even out the mixture on the plate.
3. Pick up a slice of pineapple and rest on the cinnamon sugar. Turn the slice over and ensure boat sides are well coated.
4. In a pan, on a low/medium heat, place the pineapple ring and let sit for a few minutes. The sugar will start to melt (I tend to do 4 in one go and sprinkle the remainder of the sugar mixture over the top of the slices).
5. Flip after 3/4 minutes of the sugar starting to gently bubble around the edges.
6. Serve on a plate by placing the pineapple slices down, ice cream scoop in the middle and drizzle a spread of your choice over the top/any extra cinnamon you may want.

Banana Muffins

Ingredients

1.5 cups flour
1/2 cup sugar
1 tbsp cinnamon
1.5 tsp baking powder
1.5 tsp baking soda
Pinch of salt
1 cup very ripe mashed bananas (will take about 3 bananas)
1/3 cup oil
1/3 cup milk
1/2 cup chopped leftover chocolate/chocolate chips (optional)

Recipe

1. Preheat the oven to 175°C.
2. If chopping chocolate, do so here.
3. Mash the bananas in a bowl. Once mashed and smooth, add the wet ingredients (oil and milk).
4. Mix the dry ingredients into the banana mixture: the flour, sugar, cinnamon, baking powder, baking soda and salt.
5. Top tip: when adding the baking powder and soda, aim to evenly sprinkle them across the whole mixture; don't clump it all in one and then mix it, otherwise you'll get some really tasty but flat muffins and some really high but fizzy tasting muffins.
6. Add the chocolate pieces. Mix thoroughly.
7. Prepare a cupcake tray with cases and fill each one no higher than 2/3rds of the way up.
8. Bake for 25 minutes: check they're cooked by sticking a sharp knife/ toothpick into a muffin and if it comes out clean, it's cooked all the way through. If they're not ready, leave them in for an extra 5 minutes and check again.

SMOOTHIES

1. White: Peanut Butter and Banana
2. Red: Red Berry
3. Orange: Peach and Ginger
4. Green: Apple and Spinach
5. Purple: Blueberry

Smoothies

White: Peanut Butter and Banana
1. 1 banana
2. 2 tbsp peanut butter
3. 3/4 cup milk

Red: Red Berry
1. 1 banana
2. 1 cup frozen mixed berries
3. 3/4 cup milk

Orange: Peach and Ginger
1. 1/2 cup milk
2. 1/2 tin peaches
3. 1cm fresh ginger, minced
4. Juice of two small oranges/one large

Green: Apple and Spinach
1. 1 kiwi
2. 1 banana
3. 1/2 cup chopped cucumber (a chunk roughly 2.5cm long)
4. 1 cup spinach
5. 1 green apple
6. 1/4 cup milk

Purple: Blueberry
1. 1 banana
2. 3/4 cup blueberries
3. 1/2 cup milk

THE

END